PATCHEN'S LOST PLAYS

PATCHEN'S LOST PLAYS

DON'T LOOK NOW and THE CITY WEARS A SLOUCH HAT

by Kenneth Patchen

edited and with an introduction by Richard G. Morgan

A NOEL YOUNG BOOK
Published by Capra Press, Santa Barbara
1977

Copyright © 1977 by Richard G. Morgan.
Manufactured in the United States of America.

"The City Wears a Slouch Hat" copyright ©1942 by Kenneth Patchen. "Don't Look Now" copyright ©1967 by Kenneth Patchen. All rights reserved. This book, or parts thereof, may not be reproduced in any form without written permission from the publisher.

CAUTION: These plays are the sole property of the copyright owner. All rights are strictly reserved, including professional, amateur, motion picture, television, radio, recitation, lecturing, public reading and foreign translation, and none of such rights can be exercised or used without written permission from the copyright owner. All inquiries for licenses and permissions for stock and amateur uses should be addressed to Capra Press, 631 State Street, Santa Barbara, CA 93101.

Facsimile of Patchen's original manuscript, page 6, through the courtesy of Kenneth Patchen Archive, University Library, Special Collections, University of California at Santa Cruz.

Special thanks to Joel Climenhaga.
Cover drawing by Marcia Burtt.

Library of Congress Cataloging in Publication Data
Patchen, Kenneth, 1911-1972.
Patchen's Lost plays.
"A Noel Young book."
CONTENTS: Don't look now.—The city wears a slouch hat.
I. Patchen, Kenneth, 1911-1972. The city wears a slouch hat. 1977. II. Title. III. Title: Lost plays.
PS3531.A764D6 1977   812'.5'4   77-13093
ISBN 0-88496-118-4
ISBN 0-88496-117-6 pbk.

CAPRA PRESS
631 State Street
Santa Barbara, CA 93101

This book is for Miriam

and it is for all the creatures of the world, particularly those who have been brutalized by the barbarism and cruelty of the human race; for every dog and cat now in a city pound, without love or care, awaiting a horrible death; for every animal crushed on the highways or starving in the streets of the world; for every animal tortured in scientific experiments, with no hope of an end to its suffering except a death both painful and unnecessary; for every creature killed to satisfy people's taste for flesh; for all creatures from the smallest to the largest, who have suffered or who are now suffering from human sadism, carelessness, or stupidity.

To them also is this book dedicated

CHARACTERS. MR WORTHCROFT, a business man; MRS WORTHCROFT, his wife; JOAN, their daughter; GERALD, Joan's young man, and an advertising copy writer; AUNT CLEOBEL house guest from out of town; FROGGY FENWICK, an acquaintance of Aunt Cleobel's, and a far out cat; OLD HORACE, a little ninety year old man in dinner clothes.

ACT ONE

SCENE. A tall, conventional room. Low to the baseboard are two low, heavily draped windows; there is a closed door at the back. One of the pushed back chairs at the table is overturned; a vase lies on its side near a telephone stand. Two small rugs emphasize the polish of the hardwood floor. In addition to the single globe ceiling fixture which blooms frostily at the end of a metal rod, there are several lighted table lamps standing beside neat stacks of magazines, a stuffed bird, and the romanesque bust of an industrialist. Everything to the height of the surprisingly short-looking windows appears considerably less than life size. The explanation for this, however, is simplicity itself. The room is upside down.

Drapes are undisturbed at the windows; the pictures have not fallen from the walls; the familiar objects of domicilic tranquility, chairs, table, table lamps, etc., are as though glued in place — on the floor-become-ceiling.

Only a scatter of red roses around the frosted globe, which rises to shoulder height from

From the original manuscript of "Don't Look Now."

ON THE SIDE OF THE ANGELS

"We must learn to love each other .... if one man fails to believe, then there can be no faith in the world—for all men are finally one man, you, me—we cannot stand apart from each other. I am coming into your house with my hand outstretched. I am your friend. Do not be afraid of me." —"The City Wears a Slouch Hat"

When Kenneth Patchen died in 1972 he took with him a body that had been tortured by time, physiology, and the deceptions of the medical profession in America for over thirty years. What remained were over forty books written in every literary genre, a half-dozen recordings, thousands of paintings, including his famous "painted books," countless poems, both collected and uncollected, numberless lives which had been changed by their contact with the wonder-filled world of Kenneth Patchen, and these two plays—one virtually forgotten in a library archive, the other lying quietly in a bureau drawer in his and Miriam Patchen's home in Palo Alto, California.

This is the first publication of the plays "The City Wears A Slouch Hat" and "Don't Look Now" (also called "Now You See It"). The presentation of any previously unavailable work by Patchen is of great importance. No single specimen of his writing or of his visual arts can adequately represent the range and strength of his achievement; no one poem or picture or paragraph can communicate the endless joy and the endless sorrow of his life "on the side of the angels." Though the plays can be said to have literary faults, they are faults arising from adventure rather than caution. In all his work, there is the spirit of experiment, of transcending the boundaries of particular media, ignoring the strictures and regulations of critics and literary theorists. As in his concrete and sound poetry, his poetry-prose novels, his painted books, picture-poems, papier-maché sculptures, his poetry-and-jazz readings, fables, and silkscreens, the action and content of these plays pushes at the boundaries of their form.

Though they were written almost twenty years apart they have much in common, both in theme and technique. Both plays are immersed in an atmosphere of war as it exists both in society and between individuals. Coupled with this surrounding horror is the hope that love is still possible, that it has to be possible; "we must love one another.... it is not too late to love one another." The potential for failure exists eternally alongside the potential for triumph and for wonder, here and in the rest of Patchen's work. In *The Journal of Albion Moonlight,* he writes,

> It was essential that we bring our message to the people who had lost hope in the world. It was our duty to go into the villages and cities—Our message was this: we live, we love you. Our religion was life .... now we are held here and the world will perish because no one is saying we love you, we believe in you.

And this was the message of Kenneth Patchen, from his first day as a writer to his last. He bore war and the sickness of society on his own shoulders, offering to free us from those ills by creating a world of angels and green deer, a world into which one might enter simply by listening to the music of the heart.

"The City Wears a Slouch Hat" was written in 1941. At that time, Patchen was helpless in bed for much of the time, his back in a state of semi-paralysis. This coupled with the poverty which was to continue almost unabated to the end of his life created a situation in which it is incredible that he was able to write at all. The disease carried with it fits of depression and moments of unbearable pain, and it is perhaps natural that his view carried beyond the material world to a world of beauty and wonder just outside the boundaries of the physical, a world negated by war and contemporary society but visible to the heart, and brought to life by him in his words and paintings. The play was performed only once, on the Columbia Radio Workshop (WBBM-CBS) on Sunday in New York, May 31, 1942. Sound was done by John Cage.

"Don't Look Now" was composed in 1958, during a brief physical respite in Patchen's nightmarish illness. His health soon became even worse, his few hours' daily work made possible only by a rigorous schedule of medication and the constant encouragement and ministrations of his wife Miriam, to whom all his books are dedicated, and to whom literature owes a great debt. She was a crucial part of Patchen's life and development, balancing with love the ravages of the long illness. For the moment, though, he was freed from the chains of that illness. What he saw was the sadness of isolation, of people unable to communicate, unable to embrace or approach one another on more than the most superficial level. It is of this sorrow that "Don't Look Now" was built.

The play opened in Palo Alto, California, on October 30, 1959, and was performed by the Troupe Theatre. From there it went to a forty-seat off-off-Broadway theatre in New York for a production by Threshholds which began on November 10, 1967, and ran for two months. (In the Threshholds production the play was called "Now You See It," according to Patchen's wishes, as he was not able to participate in the production and felt it would be a play different from the original.) Additional productions of

"Don't Look Now" were staged at Culver-Stockton College in Canton, Missouri, in 1968, and at Kansas State University in Manhattan, Kansas, in 1970. These two latter performances were both directed by Joel Climenhaga, a longtime friend of the Patchens.

In editing the plays, I have standardized spelling and corrected obvious typographical errors. I did not alter grammar or usage except in extreme cases where it was both an apparently inadvertent error and also an obstacle to the understanding of the passage. The source for "The City Wears a Slouch Hat" was Special Collections in the library at Northwestern University. I thank that institution in general and Russell Maylone in particular for generously permitting me to make use of it. This version of "Don't Look Now" was edited from four separate copies of that play—typescripts at the New York Public Library (Curator, Paul Myers), in the possession of Joel Climenhaga and Miriam Patchen, and the original handwritten version now housed at the University of California at Santa Cruz. I thank all those parties for making copies available to me.

Particular thanks is due to Miriam Patchen for the faith and confidence she has given me, and for whom my admiration and respect grows each moment. And as always, my deep love and appreciation to Lissa Fischer.

—Richard G. Morgan
Williamstown, West Virginia
April, 1977

DON'T LOOK NOW

THE TROUPE THEATRE PRESENTS

THE FIRST PLAY BY KENNETH

PATCHEN
WORLD PREMIERE
"DON'T LOOK NOW"
OPENING FRIDAY, OCT. 30

LIMITED ENGAGEMENT – 5 WEEKS

RESERVED SEATS FOR
"DON'T LOOK NOW" — $2.65
FOR RESERVATIONS CALL
DA 1-4220
642 HIGH STREET
PALO ALTO

DIRECTED BY PHILLIP ANGELOFF   PRODUCED BY MICHAEL DU PONT AND WALTER TESCHAN

Cast

MR. WORTHCROFT, a businessman

MRS. WORTHCROFT, his wife

JOAN, their daughter

GERALD, Joan's young man and an advertising copywriter

AUNT CLEOBEL, houseguest from out of town

FROGGY FENWICK, an acquaintance of Aunt Cleobel and a far out cat

OLD HORACE, a little 90-year-old man in dinner clothes

Act One

SCENE: *A tall, conventional room. Close to the baseboard are two low, heavily draped windows; there is a closed door at the back. One of the pushed-back chairs at the table is overturned; a vase lies on its side near a telephone stand. Two small rugs emphasize the polish of the hardwood floor. In addition to the single globe ceiling fixture which blooms frostily at the end of a metal rod, there are several lighted table lamps standing beside neat stacks of magazines, a stuffed bird, and the romanesque bust of an industrialist. Everything to the height of the surprisingly short-looking windows appears considerably less than life size. The explanation for this, however, is simplicity itself. The room is upside down.*

Drapes are undisturbed at the windows; the pictures have not fallen from the walls; the familiar objects of domicilic tranquility, chairs, table, table lamps, etc., are as though glued in place—on the floor-become-ceiling.

Only a scatter of red roses around the frosted globe, which rises to shoulder height from the flowered ceiling-become-floor, still reminds us of Newton and his equally celebrated apple. This—and of course the persons of our little drama.

It is evening.
The place, any large city.
—And to repeat: the room is upside down.

The curtain has been up perhaps two or three minutes and we have heard no sound from the occupants of the topsy-turvy room. But we have seen them reacting naturally—which is to say, frantically—to the circumstance of their sudden, and rather perplexing, imprisonment. The Worthcrofts, JOAN and GERALD, have shown greater orientation in the direction of pounding on walls, tapping on the "floor," bumping into and shouting to one another, etc., than they have for what could be described as something having a more nearly personal, or even altruistic connotation. Very different the behavior of the three others: just as frantic, and as opposite . . . concerned, intimate, touching—much warm handshaking, arm-around-shouldering, mutual and extensive dusting off of clothes, straightening of hats, etc., and all to the accompaniment of heartfelt compliments which it would be a rare pleasure to hear.

This contrast in group behavior is, if anything, underlined by several concrete instances: one could be when MR. WORTHCROFT, dashing to another wall, tumbles over FROGGY FENWICK who is living, if slowly, not to say languidly, up to his name; and another, when the same MR. WORTHCROFT, on that same occasion, angrily rises to find himself blessed with a passenger in the cheerful person of OLD HORACE.

But now JOAN, starting at one side, and GERALD, from the other, are feeling over the front wall—the one that appears invisible. As they meet, and pass, at center, MR. WORTHCROFT, with his wife beside him, makes another, even more determined, but equally futile, effort to get a handhold on the top (which seems the bottom to him) of one of the windows.

Then, as GERALD and JOAN shift their investigation to another wall, the WORTHCROFTS take their places in survey of the one at front; and just as they come together, are about to pass one another—suddenly, exactly as parts in a rundown toy, everyone freezes. They are as though turned to stone: the perpetuation of all the strangely pathetic, and perhaps even comical, attitudes of this least casual and assured of animals.

Perhaps ten, fifteen, twenty seconds go by.

Then while the others remain frozen, AUNT CLEOBEL, *who is standing near the globe, suddenly stoops, seems to pick something up, brings her arm back, takes aim at the invisible wall, lets fly—and from high up comes the splintering crash of breaking glass.*

And with it, release, motion, sound—all in a burst, a volume-up babble:

MR. WORTHCROFT:
—the hell you're doing?

JOAN:
—all this time?

MRS. WORTHCROFT:
—this would happen!

FROGGY:
Crazy!

GERALD:
—it over quietly.

OLD HORACE:
—someone else's little half-grown rowboat.

Sudden silence again.

THE WORTHCROFTS *lower their shielding arms.* FROGGY *leans his elbow on the globe.* GERALD *puts his arm around* JOAN. *The group converges on* AUNT CLEOBEL. OLD HORACE *begins to pump* MR. WORTHCROFT'S *hand up and down.*

OLD HORACE:
Nice place you have here, boy. Yes, sir! Haven't had so much fun since the mayor caught his wig in the car door.

MR. WORTHCROFT *(shaking him off)*:
All right, Cleobel! Let's have it!

AUNT CLEOBEL *(sniffing a rose)*:
I don't know what you're talking about, Jamesy.

MR. WORTHCROFT:
You know damn well what I'm talking about! What did you break that window with?

AUNT CLEOBEL *(raptly sniffing)*:
Why, I . . . oh, it could have been any number of things. Like my shoe, for instance. Women have been known to break things with their—

MR. WORTHCROFT *(to his wife)*:
That settles it! I knew she was at the bottom of this somewhere! And if ever again you invite her to this house I'll . . . I'll—And this time I mean it! I'll have no more of it, do you understand? Her and those damn loonies she keeps dragging in here!
MRS. WORTHCROFT:
Oh, shut up, James! Just because Cleobel's taste in people is maybe . . . well, a little different from yours, doesn't mean you can get away with blaming this on her, too.
MR. WORTHCROFT:
What are you talking about, "too"?
MRS. WORTHCROFT:
I'm talking about that empty-headed little thing you took to Atlantic City last week. I think you said her name was *Mr.* Cartwright. Something to do with roller castings. A very responsible position for a sixteen year old . . . with half a pound of orange lipstick where her face ought to be.
MR. WORTHCROFT:
Eighteen. And besides, it *was* her doing! *(Glaring at Aunt Cleobel.)* I was going down the boardwalk on my way to the meeting, when all of a sudden, bam! Just like that! *(He snaps his fingers.)*
MRS. WORTHCROFT:
The part about the bored walk I'll buy. *(With a snort of irritation, her husband strides to the back of the room.)*
AUNT CLEOBEL *(to Froggy)*:
My brother-in-law is accusing me of giving him some kind of post-hypnotic suggestion.
FROGGY:
Crazy.
GERALD:
Will you repeat the brand name on that again, Miss Clugget?
JOAN:
Oh, we told you all about that, Gerald. Anyway, it's nothing. Aunt Cleobel just has a habit of looking straight at a person,

sort of. I think we have something a bit more important to do than just stand around here chewing dirty linen.
GERALD:
I remember your telling me your aunt carved little polar bears out of whitewashed sweet potatoes and things like that.
MR. WORTHCROFT *(who has been pounding on the wall at left, comes angrily up)*:
What the devil's the matter with you people?
MRS. WORTHCROFT:
What's the matter with you? Do you have to shout like that? Do you think we're all deaf or something?

MR. WORTHCROFT:
Well, you damn well must be! Yelling my head off, and you don't even look 'round! Where the devil are those people who live in the next apartment?
JOAN:
You mean you were yelling just now, over there? *(Turning to look at the wall.)*
MR. WORTHCROFT:
You're damn right I was! *(To his wife.)* Now, look Helen, I warned you! If that sister of yours has been up to some more of her damn tricks with that hypnotizing stuff again—!
MRS. WORTHCROFT *(who is watching* JOAN *and* GERALD *gesturing and making shouting faces from the wall—only a few feet away)*:
Oh, shut up James! *(As* JOAN *comes up.)* We didn't hear a sound. Not a sound.
GERALD *(joining them)*:
Well, that definitely does put a new item on the expense account.
MR. WORTHCROFT *(starting back to the wall)*:
Do you mean to say that just a few fee— *(And his voice goes abruptly dead.)*
MRS. WORTHCROFT *(shouting happily after him)*:
Yes, you big overstuffed adding machine, you! We can't hear a single pompous word you're saying!

AUNT CLEOBEL:
> Now, sister Helen, that's not very kind. Jamesy may have his faults, but he's really not a bad sort. He's just not ever kind of... well, woke up inside himself.

MRS. WORTHCROFT *(as her husband approaches again)*:
> You can say that again. *(to him)*: Well, are you satisfied now?

MR. WORTHCROFT *(turning to* GERALD*)*:
> What do you make of this, Gerald?

GERALD:
> I suppose when the room... *(And he bends far to the side)* went over, it set up a kind of short-like; you know, an aberration of acoustical balance, a sort of *deviate* in reverse logistics-like.

FROGGY:
> Like. Man, you use words, they stay used. I really dig that opening movement. *(And he very slowly imitates* GERALD's *sideways action.)*

MR. WORTHCROFT *(at his tether's end)*:
> Deviate! I guess it must be catching. Wonder if it works the same when you get ou— *(His voice goes abruptly dead as he makes his way to the wall on the other side.)*
>
> *(And everyone except* FROGGY, *who is doing some head-bobbing, tongue-out tapping on the globe, is now busy exploring the acoustical eccentricities of the room.*
>
> MRS. WORTHCROFT *and* AUNT CLEOBEL *form one party;* JOAN *and* GERALD, *another; while* OLD HORACE *enjoys a stealthy lockstep at the heels of* MR. WORTHCROFT.
>
> *Presently all except these latter two return to the globe.)*

GERALD:
> Um, we'll have to stick a few feathers on that and see if she still swims upstream.

JOAN:
> Oh, Gerald, can't you talk so somebody can understand you? Just this once? For me? Will you try? Just this one time? Please!

GERALD *(very surprised)*:
> Huh?

JOAN *(moving away wearily)*:
   Oh, forget it. *(She sits down at the back wall, where* GERALD *joins her, takes her hand, talks earnestly to her bowed head.)*
MRS. WORTHCROFT *(to her sister)*:
   Tell us honestly, Cleobel. Did you have anything to do with this . . . this crazy upside down business?
AUNT CLEOBEL:
   Cross my heart, Helen. I was as surprised as anybody.
MRS. WORTHCROFT:
   Well, all right. Maybe you were. But you do seem rather light-hearted about it all.
AUNT CLEOBEL:
   And you would too, sister Helen. If you were like me, and lived your whole life long in the kind of little town I do. With everybody thinking you're kind of . . . well, silly and odd, just because you maybe don't exactly care for all the things they care for.
MRS. WORTHCROFT *(mildly)*:
   And maybe do care for a few things they kind of don't care for.
AUNT CLEOBEL:
   You know I've thought about it a lot. More than anybody could know—particularly since . . . well, since I— *(Nodding her head at* FROGGY, *who is trying it with another beat)* since I got to really thinking about people. I mean, not just this man has this job or . . . or that job; or Mrs. Bartlett across the street—remember I told you she had that pretty little peach tree cut down just so she could have a few more washlines—well, that she never once has had the time to just sit down and kind of make a face at herself. Because when we were first born—I don't mean just you and me, but the first ones—now you know there weren't any dirty, smelly factories then, or even a school, or a Greyhound bus—so maybe people didn't think it funny to fall in love with a little spotty brown dog, or dance around the yard

when it rained—or kind of not care if you never got married, or— You know what I mean, don't you, Helen?
MRS. WORTHCROFT:
I know what you mean. But I still think just because that Bartlett brat poisoned your dog, you didn't have to set up a stuffed stork right on your porch, where everytime she came out of the house she'd see it. Not a stork with crossed eyes anyway. *(Her attention is on her husband, who is pressing his ear to the wall, first in this spot, then in that; while* OLD HORACE, *his crushed top hat still tightly in place on his head, seems to be continuing his snooze against the baseboard.)* Having twenty-four children is no crime against nature, not the last I heard, at least. *(And as her husband begins to gesture frantically)* You don't suppose somebody's operating a cash register on the other side of that wall, do you? *(And she crosses to him.)*

(AUNT CLEOBEL, *seeing that* GERALD *and* JOAN *are also crossing to see what has* MR. WORTHCROFT *so excited, is about to join the group at the wall when* FROGGY *restrains her with a light hand.)*

AUNT CLEOBEL *(straight and thin in her old-fashioned clothes, complete with striped stockings)*:
Yes, Froggy?
FROGGY *(Slumped and gone under the spectacular sharoness of mostly-lapel suit, complete with unlighted cigarette and eyes)*:
Like them— *(Pointing to the earpressers.)* I mean, he's a cat, see.
AUNT CLEOBEL:
You mean Mr. Horace?
FROGGY:
Yeah, I mean, lady, I wouldn't yak you none. You dig? I wouldn't, see?
AUNT CLEOBEL:
I know you wouldn't, Froggy.
FROGGY:
He's a little old, see. I mean, most times you don't figure one that old for a swinger.

AUNT CLEOBEL:
   I know, Froggy. Most of you nice young people are . . . well, kind of young.
FROGGY:
   Yeah. So he comes on. Nice tone and all. Good light beat. *(He makes a slow motion of knocking.)* You dig?
AUNT CLEOBEL *(slowly)*:
   Oh. You mean Mr. Horace has been knocking on the wall, and they think— Oh. *(And she stops the words with her hand.)*
FROGGY:
   Like. Cool. *(He taps a slow measure on the globe.)*
AUNT CLEOBEL *(deliberating)*:
   I suppose in a way it doesn't hurt anything. Gives Jamesy something besides his ulcer to chew on. Still. He does have such an unreasonable temper. And Mr. Horace is so sweet and . . . and so kind of trusting—almost like a little pink baby with white hair.
FROGGY:
   Like you say. Squares like that, he'd do better they phoned up the fuzz.
AUNT CLEOBEL *(her gaze slowly lifting to the furniture jutting down from above)*:
   Ah! The phone . . . Excuse me, Froggy. *(And she crosses to the group at the wall.)*
   (In a moment all except OLD HORACE *are again gathered in front of the globe.)*
MR. WORTHCROFT *(to* FROGGY*)*:
   Did it ring again?
AUNT CLEOBEL *(quickly, as* FROGGY *interrupts his beat to glance at her)*:
   I told you there was only this one tiny kind of half-tinkle, like maybe something was wrong with the connection.
JOAN *(gazing up)*:
   Looks all right. The receiver hasn't fallen or anything.
MR. WORTHCROFT *(putting a cigar in his mouth)*:
   No, the only thing that's fallen are those damn roses!

MRS. WORTHCROFT:
   You're forgetting us, darling.
MR. WORTHCROFT *(looking at his wristwatch)*:
   I was expecting a call somewhere around nine-thirty. *(He holds the watch to his ear, then, after shaking it, tries again.)* Damn! What time have you got, Gerald?
GERALD *(repeating the same motions with his wristwatch)*:
   I'm afraid, the same as you, Mr. Worthcroft.
   (A general checking of wristwatches.)
MR. WORTHCROFT:
   Now what the devil do you suppose that means? Even the damned watches are stopped!
MRS. WORTHCROFT:
   Maybe it just means that time has run out for us, that's all, darling.
MR. WORTHCROFT *(irritably)*:
   Has anybody got a match? That's very funny, Helen. Especially since you're right. And I can even tell exactly when it happened. Well, I said: Has anybody got a match?
GERALD:
   I'm afraid not, Mr. Worthcroft. You see, I wanted to light a cigarette—oh, maybe fifteen minutes ago.
MR. WORTHCROFT:
   I don't give a damn how long ago it was! *(And he unbands his wristwatch and slams it down.)* Did you ask him? *(Glaring at FROGGY.)*
GERALD:
   Yes. He said he never carried matches—I believe he said he preferred his smoke cool.
FROGGY:
   Crazy.
MR. WORTHCROFT *(shaking his cigar at FROGGY)*:
   Do you know, there's a half-wit who sweeps up my office is an Einstein next to you!
FROGGY *(trying to place it)*:
   No. But maybe if you hummed a few bars, I could pick up the chorus.

(MR. WORTHCROFT *strides in disgust back to the wall where* OLD HORACE *still dozes.*)
JOAN *(to her mother)*:
So he found out about you and the Hamilton's gardener?
MRS. WORTHCROFT:
No, this was the steward on that second honeymoon cruise we took to Florence. At least I think so. The young idiot forgot to lock the cabin door. But your father came in with a big envelope full of specifications for a new-type refrigerator insulation—so, as I say, I can't really be sure he noticed anything. Funny, I can't so much as remember the color of the steward's eyes, but I even know the strand-count on the llama armpit hair they were going to use on that insulation. And they talk about dogs getting to look like their masters. Oh, let's do something! Anybody know any funny stories, or anything?
AUNT CLEOBEL:
I know a game where everybody pretends to climb a hill, and you tell what you'd most want to have when you get to the top. You know, like seeing an unusual kind of bird, or maybe even a person—say, somebody like . . . well, like one of those beautiful knights in a story. Or . . . well, you know, what each person might like to find up there. On the very top of the hill, I mean.
MRS. WORTHCROFT *(turning idly to look over at her husband)*:
That sounds almost too exciting, Cleobel. I guess Jack the Rapper is back.
AUNT CLEOBEL *(quickly, as the others turn to watch* MR. WORTHCROFT *excitedly plying his ear to the wall again)*:
Oh, I'm sure it's just something creaking or banging somewhere—you know how a house will make all kinds of strange noises at night.
GERALD *(putting a restraining hand on* JOAN'S *arm, as she moves to investigate the knocks)*:
Remember, we were surprised when your father said he'd heard knocking from the Hamilton's apartment?

JOAN:
And why not, since they're not due back from Europe for two months?

GERALD:
But that isn't why we should have been surprised. Look. This is the top room in a penthouse, right? Right. And that door . . . *(Pointing up at it.)* leads to a landing, and then you walk down a short flight of steps to the rest of your apartment.

JOAN:
So?

GERALD:
So this. On one side you have the top room of the Hamilton's, set like this one, with just the wall dividing them. And both of them sort of on an "L", stuck out from the rest of the building.

(OLD HORACE has given a tug at the brim of his crushed top hat, gotten to his feet, looked about him in surprise, and now walks forward to join them. MR. WORTHCROFT *is now alternately rapping—two, three, two, three—and pausing to listen; speeding up the process as his excitement grows.)*

JOAN:
And on the other side . . . *(Pointing to the wall at the left)* there's nobody. Nobody at all. Not even a neighbor in Europe. There's nothing, not so much as a fire escape. Why, it must be a couple hundred yards over to the next building even. So what are you getting at, Gerald?

AUNT CLEOBEL *(looking wonderingly up)*:
Gerald is right!

GERALD:
Of course I am. Don't you see? What I'm getting at is this: when you stand at the door, the Hamilton's are over there. *(Pointing in the direction of* MR. WORTHCROFT.*)* So if somebody is knocking on that wall . . . *(He pauses dramatically.)*

AUNT CLEOBEL *(quickly)*:
Oh then it just proves what I was saying. The moisture of the night air probably makes—

OLD HORACE *(putting his hand lightly on her arm)*:
   There is somebody—or *something*—knocking out there, all right. I'm a sound sleeper for my age, Miss, but not that sound. Unless I mean . . . that sound. You see, Miss, I heard it too.
FROGGY *(running his fingers rapidly down his lapels)*:
   Crazy. That's got Bird all over it!
GERALD:
   All right. We know that nobody—no person, that is—can be knocking on that wall . . .
JOAN *(turning to look about with irritable unease)*:
   Just as we also know that nobody can be standing on the ceiling of an upside down room, I suppose.
GERALD *(as he starts off to join* MR. WORTHCROFT*)*:
   Maybe we're not.
      (There is a pause.)
JOAN *(slowly)*:
   Now what did he mean by that?
MRS. WORTHCROFT *(placing her arm around her daughter)*:
   It just means that Gerald remembers the last bout of nerves you had—I think it was in your freshman year, between semesters. And we sent you to that doctor who'd only been over here a little while from Vienna.
JOAN *(brightening)*:
   And I persuaded Aunt Cleobel to go to his office with me.
AUNT CLEOBEL *(reminiscently adjusting the tall red feather on her old-fashioned hat)*:
   Passed me off as your mother.
JOAN *(laughing)*:
   And we took him down to—what's the name of that nightclub, Aunt Cleobel?
AUNT CLEOBEL:
   The Whalers' Roost.
FROGGY *(Breaking off to do a few sideways knee flexings)*:
   The most!
JOAN:
   And along about one or two— Who was it suggested

shaving off the bottom part of his beard because he kept knocking ice cubes onto the floor?

AUNT CLEOBEL:
Why, he did. I never saw a man so thirsty in all my life. Even drank part of my ginger ale.

(OLD HORACE *has moved off to the left, where with great difficulty he is unable to pry off his crushed top hat,* FROGGY *goes negligently to assist him, and together they have a quite motionful, if unsuccessful, session with it.*

GERALD *is drawing diagrams in a notebook, occasionally lifting his pen to point above, below, and to the left and right; while* MR. WORTHCROFT, *chewing grimly on his soggy cigar, stands with feet wide apart in attention beside him.*)

JOAN:
And he said when he was little he had this urge to sneak up on his father—his father was a judge, wore one of those powdered wigs and all—and tickle him right in court. So he had to keep showing us how he'd do it. *(She laughs.)* These days a lot of pretty stuffy people go to a place like that. You know, watch the funny monkeys. Anyway, it got pretty hectic.

AUNT CLEOBEL:
Remember that hoity-toity woman in the green-dyed mink. Why, she went through that snaredrum so fast, it took Charlie Manders a good couple seconds to pick up the beat on that baldheaded man who always talked through everything at the first table.

(MR. WORTHCROFT *shakes his head, throws his cigar angrily up at the ceiling-once-floor, and settles himself grimly down against the baseboard. After looking at him a moment,* GERALD *moves to join the group in front of the globe.*)

JOAN *(as* GERALD *comes up)*:
What did you mean by that 'Maybe the room isn't upside down' remark of yours?

GERALD *(lightly, putting his hand on her arm)*:
Did I say something like that? What are they doing? *(Indicating* FROGGY *and* OLD HORACE.)

AUNT CLEOBEL:
 Oh, that's what he was doing when we met him in the park.
MR. WORTHCROFT:
 What who was doing, Cleobel?
AUNT CLEOBEL:
 Why, Mr. Horace. We were walking down the path talking—on our way here—when we saw him half under this bench, trying to take his hat off. And when we couldn't either, why, we said, you come along with us.
MRS. WORTHCROFT:
 I suppose he'd had a big thirst, too.
AUNT CLEOBEL:
 Oh, no. He said it was because his head was radioactive. And that's why he couldn't—
MRS. WORTHCROFT *(interrupting)*:
 His head was what?
AUNT CLEOBEL:
 Radioactive. You know, like all those reports in the papers about cows and sheeps that had been—
MRS. WORTHCROFT *(wearily interrupting again)*:
 I know, I know, Cleobel. Happens every day. *(To* GERALD, *as she nods over at her husband.)* Is he having one of his bilious attacks again?
GERALD:
 Something like that. I told him about an idea I had that perhaps we...
JOAN *(as he thinks about saying it)*:
 Well? That perhaps we what?
GERALD *(lightly, to* AUNT CLEOBEL*)*:
 Say, how does that game of yours go again, Miss Clugget?
AUNT CLEOBEL *(brightly)*:
 Oh, it's very easy. And it's a lot of fun, too. Everybody pretends he's walking up a hill, and—
MRS. WORTHCROFT *(interrupting, and starting over to her husband)*:
 'Pretends' is the right word.
JOAN:
 What's going on, Gerald? What were you writing in that

notebook? And how come you're suddenly talking about playing games? Why, I don't think you've played a game since you were five years old.
GERALD *(feeling his way)*:
Well, you remember Stochey Brellsmith. I think you met him at Bob and Margaret's. Slight fellow with a quick way of talking. A bug on Hi-Fi and all that.
AUNT CLEOBEL:
Wasn't he your roommate—I believe, your last year at Yale?
GERALD *(surprised)*:
That's right. How'd you remember that, Aunt Cleobel?
AUNT CLEOBEL *(half-turning to watch as* MR. WORTHCROFT *gets quickly to his feet, and his wife, after rapping sharply at the wall beside them, moves swiftly across the room to repeat the action there)*:
Oh, he told me how he'd once scrambled all the inter-com systems in the administration building.
GERALD:
That's Stochey. Although he's cut all that out pretty much—you can't be a front desker at Westinghouse for three years and not—
JOAN *(breaking in, as her parents begin to converge on them from opposite sides of the room; while* FROGGY *and* OLD HORACE *turn round and round, making exaggerated gestures of pleased surprise)*:
What's Stochey whatever-his-name-is got to do with it?
MR. WORTHCROFT *(excitedly)*:
Now you can't hear a damn thing anywhere back there! *(With a sweep of his arm to the room behind them.)* You bang on the wall, shout yourself blue in the face—nothing! Not a whisper! I tell you we've damn well got to get out of here!
MRS. WORTHCROFT:
Now, James, You know what the doctor said about—
MR. WORTHCROFT *(interrupting, and beginning to pace back and forth)*:
I don't give a damn what he said! *(Pacing to the left.)* I only wish that mutton-head was—*(As his voice goes abruptly dead.)*
GERALD *(glancing at his notebook, and shaking his head)*:
This is worse than I thought.

JOAN *(with nervous impatience)*:
   Oh, for God's sake, Gerald! What's happening now?
MRS. WORTHCROFT *(soothingly)*:
   It'll be all right, Joanie.
JOAN:
   What'll be all right? Isn't this mess enough as it is! And nobody doing anything except a lot of silly tapping on the walls and strutting about with a notebook! I suppose you're working on some more of those stupid slogans of yours!
MR. WORTHCROFT *(striding into ear range again)*:
   What was all that damn double-talk you were giving me, Gerald, about dying waves or something?
GERALD *(as* FROGGY *and* OLD HORACE *come to rest negligently and smilingly, respectively, one on either side of the globe)*:
   Decaying sound waves. Stochey made a lot of experiments with stuff like that—rigged up a sound chamber in our room. I don't remember much of it, but—
MR. WORTHCROFT:
   All right. Let's have it in Amer-rican this time!
GERALD *(slowly)*:
   Well, in any language it simply means that if you once get a vacuum-area going in, say, a bucket of water—
MR. WORTHCROFT *(his voice rising)*:
   Leave out the damn bucket of water!
AUNT CLEOBEL:
   Do you mean, Gerald, like when there's a rotten apple in a basket?
GERALD:
   Something like that. Of course, it's a lot more complicated.
MR. WORTHCROFT:
   Well, uncomplicate it!
GERALD:
   Okay. It means that . . . that within a given time this room will be dead. That is, as far as sound is concerned. Those dead areas back there . . . *(Indicating the room behind and to the sides of them)* will gradually corrupt this one. And you won't have a single sound wave working—or rather, you won't be able to pick up—

MR. WORTHCROFT *(interrupting soberly)*:
   What about this 'given time' business? How long before it...? How long will it take?
GERALD *(shrugging again)*:
   Oh. I'd say—figuring on the basis of what we've seen happen to the sound in the rest of the room—that it might take a... well, a while.
JOAN *(impatiently, as she sets out to investigate for herself)*:
   I think the whole thing's crazy! You're probably all imagining it anyway. Some form of mass-hal— *(And her voice goes abruptly dead.)*
   (She can be seen tapping on the walls, on the floor; as she soundlessly calls.)
MRS. WORTHCROFT:
   And when this part goes blank too...? When we can't even hear our own shouts...?
MR. WORTHCROFT *(grimly)*:
   We'll be really stuck here. To rot in this damn... damn crazy upside down mess.
GERALD *(slowly)*:
   There is one thing.
MR. WORTHCROFT *(stopping his pacing to face around)*:
   What thing?
GERALD:
   About those games.
MR. WORTHCROFT:
   Games? What are you talking about now?
GERALD:
   It's something I remember Stochey said. It might give us more time anyway.
MR. WORTHCROFT:
   Well, come on! Does a person have to use a can opener on you every time?
JOAN *(coming up, her manner altered to one of near-panic now)*:
   What are we going to do?
GERALD *(putting his arm around her)*:
   It'll be all right now, honey.

(There is a pause. The group draws closer together.)

AUNT CLEOBEL:
  I agree with Gerald. I think it would be good to play some games. Kind of... well, relax us. And it'd make the time pass quicker.

GERALD *(smiling at her)*:
  Which is just what we don't want to do. No, I meant something quite different. You see, what we've got to do is try to keep this sound area alive for as long as we possibly can.

MR. WORTHCROFT:
  So what were you talking about games for?

GERALD:
  Oh, it doesn't have to be games. It can be anything. Anything that keeps the sound waves in motion. Singing. Talking. Reciting poems, speeches, market reports. Anything that resists the vacuum. Every second of silence means a second lost—a second nearer the time when we... when we can't make ourselves heard anymore.

MR. WORTHCROFT:
  This is on the level? Not just some goofy stuff you've read in a magazine or something?

GERALD:
  It's on the level, Mr. Worthcroft.

MR. WORTHCROFT:
  Well, come, somebody! One, Two, Three...

MRS. WORTHCROFT:
  I see a tree.

AUNT CLEOBEL:
  And in the tree there is a bird with golden wings.

GERALD:
  Smoking a huge meerschaum pipe.

FROGGY *(leaning forward, lazily alert)*:
  Crazy.

MR. WORTHCROFT *(as there is a slight pause)*:
  Well? Anything! Come on! Crazy. Hazy. Eat a daisy.

OLD HORACE:
  I love you sir. You look just like an early playmate of mine. We used to dance all around the schoolyard together.
MR. WORTHCROFT (*grabbing* OLD HORACE *by the hands and jumping him 'round and 'round*):
  Fine. Fine. I remember the incident very well. Took off my socks because they started to smell. One, two, three, four . . .
MRS. WORTHCROFT:
  I went to the jewelry store.
JOAN:
  And there I bought a ring.
GERALD:
  Which caused me to sing.
MR. WORTHCROFT (*suiting the action to the word*):
  "In the shade of the old ap-ple tree, da da da da da da da dee." Come on, somebody! You used to know some songs, Helen. (*He lets go of* OLD HORACE, *who promptly falls to a sitting position.*) Oh, I'm sorry. Hurt yourself?
OLD HORACE (*looking up happily*):
  No, but I just remembered something.
MR. WORTHCROFT (*quickly picking up the tempo of urgency again*):
  Come on! Come on! Did you hear what he said?
GERALD:
  He said he'd just remembered something.
MRS. WORTHCROFT:
  That's what he said. That's exactly what he said.
AUNT CLEOBEL:
  And he's got a radioactive head.
JOAN (*her heart not in it*):
  And when somebody with a radioactive head remembers something . . .
MR. WORTHCROFT:
  It should be worth remembering! Come on! Come on! Ask him what it was he remembered. It's not every day you meet a man with a radioactive head! How old are you, Mr. . . . er—
AUNT CLEOBEL:
  Mr. Horace.

OLD HORACE *(getting to his feet)*:
Just call me Winnie.
MR. WORTHCROFT:
Did you hear that? He said to call him Winnie! I'm pleased to know you, Winnie. What line of business were you in?
OLD HORACE:
I owned the biggest diaper-wash in all Philadelphia. *(Drawing himself up proudly.)* Be ninety-one the twelfth and fourteenth of next February.
MR. WORTHCROFT:
Did you hear that? He had the biggest diaper-wash in all Philadelphia!
OLD HORACE *(basking in the attention)*:
And I'll be ninety-one the twelfth and fourteenth of next February.
FROGGY *(moving to stand near him)*:
Man, you deserve at least two birthdays! Like when a cat gets as old as you—and still comes on!
MR. WORTHCROFT:
Right! This young man is absolutely right! Winnie, tell me something. Besides being the biggest diaper washer in Philly, and having two birthdays because you're so old, is there anything else special about you? I mean, did you ever go into stocks or anything like that?
OLD HORACE:
Nope, but I was in vaudeville for a spell. Only that ain't why I have two birthdays.
MR. WORTHCROFT:
No? Then, tell me this, Winnie: Why *do* you have two birthdays?
OLD HORACE:
'Cause I was born twins. And one of us died. *(He pauses for effect.)* Nobody ever knew which one of us it was!
MR. WORTHCROFT *(mechanically working to keep the soundwaves alive)*:
I see. So you took over the extra birthday. I suppose that's a routine from your vaudeville days?

OLD HORACE:
   Oh, no. That's the truth. In my act I just used my head.
MR. WORTHCROFT *(showing weariness with the forced conversation)*:
   And don't forget, he's got one that's radioactive.
JOAN *(showing impatient strain)*:
   Oh, this is getting more ridiculous by the minute! If you have to do this . . . this silly business of Gerald's about the sound waves, then why don't we . . . oh, I don't know, recite Shakespeare or . . . or Shakespeare.
MR. WORTHCROFT:
   Fine! Fine! Let me see. "Fourscore and seven years ago our fathers brought forth upon this continent a new nation, conceived in liberty, and dedicated to . . . to—er . . ."
MRS. WORTHCROFT:
   Julius Sandberg, Act 1, scene 3.
GERALD:
   "When that I was and a little tiny boy,
   With hey, ho, the wind and the rain,
   A foolish thing was but a toy,
   For the rain it raineth every day.
   But when I came to man's estate,
   With hey, ho, the wind and the rain,
   'Gainst knaves and . . . and—?
   Well, that's it. Surprised I even remembered that much.
   (OLD HORACE *is bent low, while* FROGGY *closely examines his crushed top hat.*)
AUNT CLEOBEL:
   Oh, that was real nice, Gerald. You say things very nicely. Almost as well as the minister at home. I remember one thing our old mailman used to recite:
   "O the miller's mill-dog lay at the mill-door,
   And his name was Little Bingo.
   B with an I, I with an N, N with a G, G with an O,
   And his name was Little Bingo.
   And the miller he bought a cask of ale,
   And he called it right good Stingo.
   S with a T, T with an I, I with an N, N with a G,

G, with an O,
And he called it right good Stingo."
Sometimes in the winter, or if it was raining real hard, I'd invite him in for a cup of tea, and some of those little peppermint-chip cookies I always bake for the holidays. Anyway, it went on and on. Finally, it ended with him having sixteen wives, and sailing up some river looking for a king's daughter who was supposed to be so beautiful it would just kind of bowl him right over. Oh, he was such a nice man. I think he was one of the best mailmen we ever had.

MRS. WORTHCROFT:
With sixteen wives he'd have to be.

AUNT CLEOBEL *(distracted by a slow-motion gesture from* FROGGY*)*:
Yes, Froggy? *(And she crosses to him and* OLD HORACE.*)*

FROGGY *(speaking as though to himself)*:
Like, you see, once this buddy of mine . . . him and me, well, we weren't making it. Spooksville everything we did. You know, we'd tell a guy: "Meet us at maybe 35th and Lexington." These shirts in the window, like with these great big white buttons, the size of little saucers . . . green and pink stripes on sort of a mousey brown. Forty bucks. We'd be standin' there. No awning or nothin', and like it starts to rain. So the guy doesn't show. Like all the time the cabs are stoppin' and startin'—only we just stand there, like all those neon lights, and the shirts get to look like somebody's splashin' blood on them. An' my buddy gets the coughs again like I'd been up to this place in the mountains to see him—you know, the big glassed-in porch bit, an' all around, these big fir trees with snow on them. An' everybody spits into a little paper envelope. So I—well, this was later—I got in the habit of goin' back up there to see this chick by the name of Virginia. Like my buddy maybe could sit in once in a while, he couldn't make it—like in a way nobody liked the style he had—like all they'd comment was: "He really comes on when there's just a few cats around." Like the truth was, he was blowin' a new horn—and it

scared them. So at first he got the coughs because he couldn't get onto nothin' steady; then he couldn't make it because he had the coughs. Like the jazz scene—so you do the crummy show tunes, you make out like the blues is some form of music....
AUNT CLEOBEL *(as* FROGGY, *head bowed, shows no sign of going on)*:
But, Froggy, what about those shirts? Did you ever get one?
FROGGY *(far away)*:
And, later I'd sit on that big glassed-in porch with Virginia and the fir trees with the snow on them—like, you know, I got to hate those trees, I got so I wanted to run up there and kick all the snow off them ... you know, big piles of white buttons on the ground. And I'd talk to her stuff that ... well, I don't know—but like I say, this was later—I told her about a dog I had once—but I never told her how I got one of those shirts for my buddy—you know, like how I pawned his horn to get it. Yeah, like the car hit him never stopped—I mean Jeff, my little yellow-eared mutt—came right over the curb for him too. So I figured it was somehow like that with my buddy, and I got him the shirt—but I didn't go the funeral. *(He pauses.)* You know, I'd go see if she's still up there, only ... well, I don't know, maybe like it's all those trees ... you know, all those trees.
JOAN *(into the silence)*:
Please. Freeze. Sneeze.
GERALD *(after a moment)*:
Sure. Bees. Bonnets. Best.
JOAN:
Worst. Cursed. Nursed. Mrs. Ester Thompson.
GERALD:
Huh? Who's she? Who's Mrs. Ester Thompson?
JOAN:
Do you remember her, mother?
MRS. WORTHCROFT:
Ester Thompson? Was she someone in your class?
JOAN *(shaking off* GERALD's *hand, and turning to her father)*:
Daddy, do you remember her?

GERALD (*as* MR. WORTHCROFT *shrugs uncomfortably*):
   All right, Joan. So what if they don't remember her? A lot of trees in a lot of woods don't necessarily end up on the table as toothpicks.
AUNT CLEOBEL (*gently to* GERALD, *as* JOAN *turns away from them*):
   Now, Gerald, this is important. Don't irritate Joanie with your advertising slang.
GERALD:
   What? Oh. All right. Only lately, seems as if—(*Breaking off, and putting his arm around* JOAN.) Look, honey—
JOAN (*very quietly*):
   She loved me. She was the first person ever to ... to ... (*Collecting herself with great effort:*) But it doesn't matter now. No, not really. (*With assumed lightness:*) I'll recite something. Yes, I remember something that Mrs. Thompson used to sing to me. (*Very quietly:*)
   "I know moon-rise, I know star-rise,
   I lay this body down.
   I walk in the moonlight, I walk in the starlight,
   To lay this body down."
MRS. WORTHCROFT (*crossing quickly to* JOAN):
   Oh, baby, of course I remember. I'm so sorry. (*With her arm around* JOAN, *to her husband:*) James. When we were living in Westport—Ester Thompson. Her little girl died the summer she came to work for us. Wait a minute—yes, that's right, her brother was a famous athlete, a runner—
MR. WORTHCROFT (*breaking in*):
   Oh sure. Sure, I remember. Only he wasn't a trackman. Let me see—basketball? Baseball?
AUNT CLEOBEL (*interrupting quickly*):
   You see, Joan? They do remember. I knew they would.
MR. WORTHCROFT:
   I got it! Football, that's what it was. Why, sure, I used to show her my scrapbooks. Yeah, a real nice woman. (*Thinking:*) And there was something else too ....
MRS. WORTHCROFT (*to* JOAN):
   She had a beautiful voice. And such a nice warm personality.

MR. WORTHCROFT:
> That's right! That's what it was. She used to want me to sing that Yale song—and I'd tell her that no self-respecting Harvard man—

MRS. WORTHCROFT *(wearily)*:
> James, please.

MR. WORTHCROFT:
> What's the matter? It's been a long, long time since you looked at my scrapbooks.

AUNT CLEOBEL:
> Joan and I were going through them just the other night.

MR. WORTHCROFT *(somewhat doubtfully)*:
> You were? Well. Surprised that they haven't been thrown out.

MRS. WORTHCROFT:
> Oh James. Do you have to be told all the time?

MR. WORTHCROFT:
> Told what?

MRS. WORTHCROFT:
> Nothing.

JOAN:
> You were... I mean, well, —Daddy, I'm always bragging about you.

MR. WORTHCROFT *(quietly)*:
> Yeah, I guess I was at that. All-American two years running.

JOAN:
> Not just that, Daddy.

MR. WORTHCROFT:
> Sure. *(Soberly:)* You know, it's kind of... well, sometimes I wish I could sort of make up for— *(As* MRS. WORTHCROFT's *hand touches his shoulder—repeats:)* Yes, there are times a man—even a man like me— yeah, a man wishes he could have... well, *(looking through wallet.)* What is mine? What belongs just to me? Ah, my social security number—that's mine! Nobody else can claim that! It's got character, dimension, psychological depth—it's something individual, full of meaning— of course it's just a number— but it's something personal to me—no other over-middle-aged

male, white caucasian, upper income bracket— oh hell! *(Lifts up another card.)* Ah, and here's another! My driver's license . . . *(Thumps chest.)* Y7803—no, it's a 2! Y7802— That's me! My essence, my own individual little numbered self— *(As he lifts up a paper, voice takes on edge)* Like a convict—*(*MRS. WORTHCROFT *leans in sorrow against him. And now he speaks with quietly controlled, distant dignity:)* And here's another item, an item that distinguishes me from kind. Not a number this time, but a piece of paper—just a piece of cheap writing paper. *(As he says next line,* MRS. WORTHCROFT *slowly raises her face.)* It's in the handwriting of my father, but the words are by someone else. You see, my father was a corporation lawyer—at one time he represented half the textile mills in New England— a rich, powerful man— and when he died, he left me a lot of money. And . . . and this— *(Raising the piece of yellow notepaper.)* My father was what you'd call a—well, what ruthless, cynical pillars of society are usually called. *(Pauses.)* Well, just before he died, he copied this out . . . and, and left it in an envelope for me. *(Begins quickly to read—then settles to grave, simple, undeclamatory pace):*

"April 9, 1927
He is a worker,
from his boyhood a skilled worker, lover of work,
with a good job and pay,
a bank account, a good and lovely wife,
two beautiful children and a neat little home
at the verge of a wood . . .

"He is a heart, a faith, a character, a man;
a man who gave all, who sacrificed all
to the cause of liberty and to his love for mankind:
money, rest, mundane ambition,
his own wife, his children, himself,
and his own life.

"I felt small at the presence of his greatness
and found myself compelled to fight back

from my eyes the tears
and quinch my heart—
troubling to my throat to not weep before him:
this man called thief and assassin and doomed.

"But Sacco's name will live in the hearts of the people
and in their gratitude when Katzmann's bones
and yours will be dispersed by time;
when your name, his name, your laws, institutions,
and your false god are but a dim remembering
of a cursed past in which man was wolf to other man . . .

"If it had not been for this thing
I might have lived out my life
talking at street corners to scorning men.
I might have died, unmarked, unknown, a failure.
Now we are not a failure.
This is our career and our triumph. Never in our
    full life could we hope to do such work
for tolerance, for justice, for man's understanding
of man, as now we do by accident.
Our words, our lives, our pains—nothing!

"The taking of our lives—lives of a good shoemaker
    and poor fishpeddler—
all! That last moment belongs to us—
that agony is our triumph."

MRS. WORTHCROFT *(interrupting)*:
  Now James, don't forget that you're a self-respecting Harvard man.

MR. WORTHCROFT *(with equal lightness)*:
  Yeah, that's right. Let's see . . . how's that song go. *(Sings "We're Poor Little Sheep"—joined in "Baa, baa, baa." After noisy applause,* AUNT CLEOBEL *begins to hum "He's Got the Whole World in His Hands." Then* MRS. WORTHCROFT *begins to sing "He's Got the Little Bitty Babies in His Hands," etc.*

    And JOAN, *very moved, goes to back of room, where she is joined and consoled by* GERALD.*)*

MR. WORTHCROFT:
All right somebody! Let's keep this thing going! Once I knew a man named Bill.
MRS. WORTHCROFT:
And so I booted him down the hill.
GERALD:
That's an idea. Let's do that game of Aunt Cleobel's. Going up the hill. Hip! Hip! *(And he begins vigorous climbing steps from a standing position.)* Oh, what do I want to see when I reach the top of the hill?
MR. WORTHCROFT *(beginning his stationary climb)*:
You want to see an elephant.
GERALD *(making only half-hearted climbing steps)*:
Playing a Picasso guitar.
MRS. WORTHCROFT *(falling into luke-warm step)*:
A sickly green elephant, with three faces all pointed in opposite ways, and all six mouths just crammed with dollar bills. The prettiest damn elephant you ever saw outside the Modern Museum.
AUNT CLEOBEL *(coming up with* FROGGY *and* OLD HORACE*)*:
Wait! Stop for a minute ... *(As the climbers slow their steps.)* That's not the way you play it! You have to be serious! Each person must say what he truly wants to—
MR. WORTHCROFT *(beginning a rapid standing-step again)*:
What the devil difference does that make? Come on, Joan, Helen, Gerald! I am climbing up the hill!
AUNT CLEOBEL *(tugging at his sleeve)*:
It makes a great deal of difference! If you aren't serious about it, you'll spoil all our chances of getting out of here!
MR. WORTHCROFT *(halting his climb again)*:
All right. If it's that all-fired important to you, then you show us how to do the damn thing!
AUNT CLEOBEL:
I certainly will. But first Mr. Horace is going to show us his trick.
MR. WORTHCROFT:
Trick? You mean magic or something? Because if it is, it's

out. We've got to keep talking ... clapping our hands ... anything to make noise.

AUNT CLEOBEL *(turning to* FROGGY *and* OLD HORACE*)*:
Don't you worry, Jamesy. Mr. Horace says it will work in fine.

FROGGY:
You're right. Like now ...

OLD HORACE *(smiling happily)*:
Any time. You remember I forgot how to take my hat off. So all he has to do is push down right there on top. *(Indicating with crooked arm.)*

AUNT CLEOBEL *(her thin, striped, stockinged legs beginning to move up and down)*:
Wait till I give you the signal, Froggy. Now. Everybody. *(The others begin their movement of climbing; but she waits for the rhythm to pick up.)* And everybody be serious. Ready, Froggy? (*FROGGY is poised to press the release-device on* OLD HORACE's *top hat.)* Now, everybody! *(Raising her voice:)* I am climbing the hill! *(The others repeat it after her.)* And on the top— *(They repeat it.)* Go, Froggy!

(FROGGY *presses down:* OLD HORACE *sweeps off his top hat with a low, flourishing bow— and "The Battle Hymn of the Republic" glories forth ... to the driving beat of a keyed-up Dixieland band!*

While —after a moment's adjustment: FROGGY *at first with dismayed fingers to his forehead; the others with normal reactions of surprise—all of them, including the still hat-flourishing* OLD HORACE, *march in climbing in step about the globe, shouting:)* A door! A star! Peace! Peace! Peace for all men! Peace! No more hatred! No more fear! No more despair! No more war! *(etc., etc.)*

ACT TWO

SCENE: MR. WORTHCROFT, AUNT CLEOBEL, *and* GERALD *are very slowly circling in front of the globe. Their movements are mechanical, their steps almost dragging, as the momentum of the parade-feeling gradually dissipates itself.* MRS. WORTHCROFT *and* JOAN *have already lost contact with the original group-excitement, and stand disspiritedly to the left;* FROGGY *and* OLD HORACE, *at the back right, out of the sound range, are together giving the battered top hat a this way and that, inside and out, examination.*

Everything is slowed: What little rhythm there is, is uncertain, jerky, indecisive; its curve downward. There is no music.

MR. WORTHCROFT:
Hip. Hip. Hip. Hooray.
GERALD:
As the snows of yesterday.
AUNT CLEOBEL:
I hope to see an angel beating a drum.
MR. WORTHCROFT:
Drum. Drum. Drum.
GERALD:
Drum. Drum. Drum-drum. Don't bother to knock, just you come.
AUNT CLEOBEL:
I hope to see a red bird blowing a horn.
GERALD:
"The sheep's in the meadow—"
MR. WORTHCROFT:
—"the cow's in the corn." *(calling to his wife and daughter:)* Well, come on, you two! Helen, you should have no trouble thinking of things to say. You certainly never did when it meant nothing. Hip! Hip!
MRS. WORTHCROFT:
I can think of a lot I could say. But I don't imagine you'd be too happy hearing it.
AUNT CLEOBEL:
I hope to see a great snowwhite horse playing a flute.
GERALD:
Toot. Toot. Toot-toot. Don't just give me the round number, give me its square root.

MR. WORTHCROFT *(across to his wife)*:
   Say anything you damn well please. Only help us keep this going. Gerald says if we hit it hard enough, we might even get this damn thing to working the other way.
GERALD:
   That's right. I remember once Stochey figured how, with a system of buzzers rigged to go off every half-second, he could unfreeze the vacuum area by about twenty-twenty-five percent; and by increasing the buzzer speed to twice that—
JOAN *(interrupting, her voice sharp with nerves)*:
   I think you all must be mad! Vacuum areas! Decaying sound-waves! What did we do before, before all this nonsense started? When we *could* be heard! We banged on the walls! We yelled! We stamped! We howled! And what happened? Did anyone come? Did anyone hear us? No! No, we're still locked up in this crazy, upside down box of a room! And we'll probably never get out! And all you can do is . . . is—*(And with a suppressed cry, she turns and runs to the wall at left, slumps down, cradles her head on her lifted knees. In a moment* GERALD *is beside her, his arm around her shoulder.)*
MRS. WORTHCROFT *(looking after them)*:
   Well. Shall we continue our little game? Anybody know any interesting stories, Mother Goose Rhymes, riddles, snappy sayings? Come on, James. Why, you were practically the life of the party for a while there. I thought maybe you'd swallowed some Miltown backwards.
FROGGY *(coming slowly up with* OLD HORACE*)*:
   That's it! That's it! Backwards!
MRS. WORTHCROFT:
   Go on, James. Keep the little white ball rolling. Ask our young friend if that's how he takes it. Though offhand, I'd guess it more likely that Miltown takes him.
      (MR. WORTHCROFT *walks off to the right wall, leans against it: his back to them.)*
AUNT CLEOBEL:
   Now, sister Helen, I know you're overwrought, but that's no excuse for—

MRS. WORTHCROFT *(interrupting lightly, patting her sister's arm)*:
I know, Aunt Cleobel. Froggy is one of your very favorite people. And I can't say I blame you. In fact, I think the next time you go to that crazy village joint of yours—
AUNT CLEOBEL *(interrupting in her turn)*:
It's not a crazy joint, Helen; not like you mean, anyway. It's all soft-dark and kind of... well, sort of like in a dream. Candles in pretty bottles on the tables, and everyone's so... so relaxed and friendly. Why, don't you remember, Helen, that's how I met Froggy. I mean that part about friendly...
MRS. WORTHCROFT *(lightly)*:
The part about relaxed will get by without a salestalk.
AUNT CLEOBEL:
I wasn't giving you any salestalk, Helen. It was a Tuesday night, and I was on my way here from the library. I was walking down one of those funny crooked little streets.
FROGGY *(to* OLD HORACE, *as they both grasp a brim of the old top hat)*:
It can't hurt it none, man! Look. Like I'm your father.
MRS. WORTHCROFT:
Who knows, maybe he is at that. They've certainly got the right room for it.
AUNT CLEOBEL:
Anyway, I got lost, and I went in through this doorway—it didn't look anything special: just a little sign in red lights, and kind of grillfront-like— I start in this little room-like, to use the phone, you know...
FROGGY:
Just one time, man. It don't work, you can put it back right side front.
OLD HORACE:
Sure, and if it blows a fuse or something it won't be no skin off your head!
MRS. WORTHCROFT:
And much to your great surprise, after you get in that little room-like, you discover that no provision has been made for little boys who might want to use the phone. But lo! combing his hair at the mirror, stands a knight in shining armor—or, it might be better to say he just kind of comes on

real cool-like. And so off on his great snowwhite steed you go, arriving safe on your door-step—with a whole wonderful new world opened to your enraptured gaze, like.

(JOAN *and* GERALD *are looking idly over, their fingers intertwined;* MR. WORTHCROFT, *an unlighted cigar in his mouth, is leaning back against the wall, and from time to time, he, too, glances over to the group before the globe.*)

AUNT CLEOBEL:
Oh, Helen, you always pretend to be so cynical.

MRS. WORTHCROFT *(again lightly)*:
You've got the wrong word, Cleobel. Try 'envy', of . . . oh, I don't know. *(Looking above her; and with the light tone gone.)* A while ago I closed my eyes, and I couldn't for the life of me picture this room in any other way than the way it is right now. I wonder, did Gerald have any theory about the sky . . .? Whether it's still above there, over our heads . . .? *(Slowly, half to herself.)* You know, it must be ten years since I looked at the sky. Nobody could prove by me that it's still up there.

AUNT CLEOBEL:
It's still up there, Helen. Things like people and the sky—the big, important things—they don't change. Only sometimes we kind of lose sight of what makes them important.

MRS. WORTHCROFT *(lightly again, as she turns to look over at* FROGGY *and* OLD HORACE*)*:
I'll buy the part about the sky, anyway. *(Across to them.)* How about some more music?

OLD HORACE:
Yep. She's backwards this trip. If a fuse blows . . . well, reckon I'm only young once.

MRS. WORTHCROFT:
You're forgetting your two birthdays.

FROGGY:
All set?

OLD HORACE:
Let 'er rip, sonny!

(FROGGY *presses on the release-device;* OLD HORACE *very cautiously lifts his top hat—and this time the music is modern jazz; tense, the patterns held in, thinned to breaking . . . cool.*)

FROGGY (*stiffening to attention, his shoulders beginning slightly to move*):
Aaah! A-a-a-h!

OLD HORACE (*making to put his hat on*):
My head's starting to feel all cool and sort of goose pimply!

FROGGY (*gently taking the hat from him and sailing it off towards the back of the room*):
Easy, dad. Like if you're happy, it comes on real sad.

(MR. WORTHCROFT, JOAN *and* GERALD, *converge slowly on the group before the globe.*)

MR. WORTHCROFT:
Now what's going on?

AUNT CLEOBEL (*slowly snapping her fingers and smiling with pleasure*):
This is that wonderful music I told you about. And everybody gets so kind of dreamy and far away.

MRS. WORTHCROFT:
Like.

GERALD:
I remember Stochey had a lot of records that sounded like that.

JOAN:
Isn't anybody going to do anything to get us out of here!

OLD HORACE:
Fellow in the act ahead of me used to lose his rent money in maybe some blackjack, he'd set fire to his hotel room. Maybe even get a couple watches off the firemen on his way out.

MR. WORTHCROFT (*turning to pace back and forth*):
That's a great idea! And I can't even light my damn cig— (*His voice goes abruptly dead.*)

GERALD:
We're losing ground. The sound area's beginning to close in. We've got to make noise! Be too bad if the 5:23 arrives at say, 4:06.

MRS. WORTHCROFT:
   Or never, say, gets here at all.
AUNT CLEOBEL:
   This would be wonderful music to play our game by!
MR. WORTHCROFT (*pacing past*):
   No more of that damn goofy hill-climbing stuff for—(*And his voice goes abruptly dead on the other side.*)
GERALD:
   Well, whatever we do, we better make it loud and fast and soon. It won't matter much where we file it if we're working on a dead account.
JOAN:
   Oh, I think you've all lost your senses! What possible difference can it make whether we have five minutes or five hours, if all we do is stand around talking like a bunch of backward imbeciles!
AUNT CLEOBEL (*putting her hand on* JOAN'S *arm*):
   Listen to the music, Joanie. See how kind of like it's trying to tell us that—
JOAN (*interrupting, her voice raised*):
   Aunt Cleobel, can you really hypnotize people?
MR. WORTHCROFT (*pacing past again*):
   Can she? I think she's already—(*His voice goes abruptly dead.*)
MRS. WORTHCROFT:
   That's an idea, Cleobel. If you only knew how I've been wanting a drink!
AUNT CLEOBEL (*turning to watch* FROGGY *doing his slow-motion flexings*):
   You know I never do it except to... well, make people happier or... or better—to kind of let them get through themselves-like.
MRS. WORTHCROFT:
   You're putting the glass right in my hand.
JOAN:
   Please, Aunt Cleobel!
AUNT CLEOBEL:
   Well. It's not really hypnotizing. I don't believe in anyone

doing that unless he knows all the medical in and outs. It
could hurt somebody if it's just done—
JOAN *(interrupting with tense impatience)*:
Then what do you do? And if it can't hurt anybody, why
don't you do it, Aunt Cleobel?
AUNT CLEOBEL *(hesitating)*:
Well. I don't know what it could be called. It only works
when people are . . . well, kind of . . . well, in need of it.
JOAN:
In need of what?
GERALD:
We better lower the tires down to the road, and let the gas
pedal worry about getting out of the floorboard.
AUNT CLEOBEL *(to* OLD HORACE*)*:
Can you bring the tempo up, Mr. Horace?
OLD HORACE *(grasping his nose)*:
Just you say when, Miss! Why, sometimes I'd get those little
white dogs jumping so fast, they'd melt away right in the air!
AUNT CLEOBEL *(as* MR. WORTHCROFT *halts beside his wife)*:
I suppose it's love.
MR. WORTHCROFT:
You suppose what's love?
AUNT CLEOBEL:
What people need.
MR. WORTHCROFT:
I think what we need is to damn-well get out of here!
MRS. WORTHCROFT:
It might be the same thing, darling.
GERALD:
We're going to try another game, sort of, Mr. Worthcroft.
The dead area's moving in too fast.
MR. WORTHCROFT:
Well, what the devil are we waiting for! Let's get on with it!
AUNT CLEOBEL:
I won't have to do it to all of you. Or, I should say, I won't
have to let all of you do it to yourselves.

MR. WORTHCROFT:
What is this? Are we guessing riddles now?
MRS. WORTHCROFT:
That's what we *have* been doing, James dear.
AUNT CLEOBEL:
Ready, Mr. Horace? *(As he nods yes.)* Then turn it up. *(*OLD HORACE *elaborately twists his nose: the music comes on again with the beat quickened and tense.)* Now. All of you concentrate. *(She pauses; continues slowly.)* First on a flower. Think of its color, its fragrance, the shape of its leaves, everything about it. But—and this is the important thing—you must think of it without giving it a name.
(There is a pause.)
MR. WORTHCROFT:
How can anybody think of a flower without having a name for it?
AUNT CLEOBEL:
You have to kind of invent one, James. Or, I should say, you have to kind of let it invent itself in your head-like.
FROGGY *(flexing about in oblivious fellowship)*:
It's got an orange-grey on one side, and reddish green on the other. Like it smells—
AUNT CLEOBEL:
Oh, you just say it to yourself, Froggy. And anyway, I don't think you need to do it.
OLD HORACE *(doing knee bends)*:
I remember another fellow had an act where everybody in the first row would have a plant grow up out of their head.
GERALD *(with exaggerated decisiveness)*:
All right, Aunt Cleobel, I've got mine thought of. Am I supposed to be in a trance now?
AUNT CLEOBEL:
No, Gerald, that's just the first thing. And you won't be in a trance. Is everybody ready for the next one? *(They nod.)* All right. There are two more. *(She pauses.)* The first is a child. Do just as you did with the flower. Concentrate hard. Imagine every little detail. The expression of his face. The way he smiles. The way he walks. Everything.

MRS. WORTHCROFT:
   I gather this little boy has clothes on?
AUNT CLEOBEL:
   That doesn't matter. The important thing is the child part. And it doesn't have to be a boy. *(She pauses.)* And the third one— [most] people can do the two together easier than one at a time— for the [third one] you just concentrate on yourself.
   (There is a pause.)
MR. WORTHCROFT:
   On ourselves? How the devil can a person imagine himself!
MRS. WORTHCROFT:
   And remember, without a name, darling. That means no power-steering, no superheterodyne transmission; 2,000 sq. ft. of freezing area, no inner-spring trust funds—
MR. WORTHCROFT *(interrupting)*:
   All right! All right! I suppose you can do it with no trouble at all?
MRS. WORTHCROFT:
   God knows, it'll at least be fun trying. *(To* GERALD.*)* What stumps me is trying to get any clear picture of myself standing upside down on the ceiling. Like you said you thought we might be.
JOAN *(turning quickly to* GERALD*)*:
   Upside down on the ceiling! *(Her voice rising with nerves.)* Oh, these horrible, horrible jokes! *(Beginning to beat on his chest with her fists.)* I can't take any more! I tell you, I can't! I can't!
MRS. WORTHCROFT *(quietly to Aunt Cleobel)*:
   I think maybe you better take a quick look through that do-it-yourself soul-building kit of yours, and see if down in the small print it had any bright ideas for the cure of simple hysterics.
AUNT CLEOBEL *(gently but authoritatively turning Joan about to face her)*:
   Joan, honey, do you trust me? Do you believe I would do anything to hurt you?
JOAN:
   I don't know! I don't know! This is all so . . . awful!

AUNT CLEOBEL *(raising her left hand)*:
  Look at my ring, Joanie.
JOAN:
  You have no ring! You're all trying to—
AUNT CLEOBEL *(interrupting gently, as the others stand very still)*:
  See, Joanie. Do you see how the stone sparkles? *(She moves her hand slowly from side to side.)* Tell me what you see, Joanie.
JOAN *(haltingly)*:
  Why, it's ... it's the most beautiful ring? The stone shines like ... like a beautiful star.
AUNT CLEOBEL *(moving her ringless hand so the others may see it)*:
  See. See how it shines. See—without blemish or flaw—and it was shining, shining just as now, before ever the first man was born into this world. Just as it will go on shining if ever the time should come that man and all his works disappear from the world.
  (There is a pause; and the music lowers in volume.)
MRS. WORTHCROFT *(wonderingly)*:
  It's a wedding ring.
MR. WORTHCROFT *(bending to look at it)*:
  And it not only shines like a star, it *is* a star!
GERALD *(very slowly)*:
  I feel like I did when I was five or six and realized for the first time that I was ... was living inside myself, and that nobody else was there. And that ... that, in some different sort of way, everybody else was living there too.
FROGGY *(taking* AUNT CLEOBEL'S *hand and gently studying it)*:
  When I got to school and they kept telling us stuff that nobody could live in, I thought, if it doesn't matter, then make sure it doesn't matter in any way they can get their hands on. Like you don't like dogs, don't spend your life trying to live and talk like one. *(And he releases her hand as the others stand very still.)*
  (There is a pause; and the music comes up again.)
OLD HORACE:
  'Nother fellah had an act anybody in the audience says something like: A man was building his house on the bank

of a river—why, he'd right away take that and he'd work up a story out of it. Blind old fellow with sandals on his feet.
AUNT CLEOBEL (*moving back to rest her hand on the globe, while the others stand before her in a circle*):
There was a man built his house on the edge of a dark forest.
MR. WORTHCROFT:
And he felt lonely in his house, and he went out and he met a young woman carrying a basket of big red apples.
MRS. WORTHCROFT:
So they went back to the house together, and they sat down by the fire and she said . . .
(*There is a pause. The music lowers in volume again.*)
JOAN:
You're paying more attention to the apples than you are to me.
GERALD:
Apples? What apples? Oh, you mean *these* apples?
JOAN:
I think I hear little Johnny crying. I'll go see if his formula's warmed up.
GERALD (*wiping his forehead*):
Whew! I don't see how time can get through that thick forest so fast!
OLD HORACE:
And pretty soon little Johnny built a house for himself. Only his house was further away from the dark forest.
MRS. WORTHCROFT:
And further away from the bright stars.
MR. WORTHCROFT:
And they stopped feeling afraid of the thunder and lightening.
FROGGY:
Like you could say, they stopped feeling almost anything.
AUNT CLEOBEL:
Because they had fallen out of love.

MRS. WORTHCROFT:
And what living went on in their houses, they let the furniture do.
GERALD:
Before long, books knew and cared more about them than they did.
(Medium beat)
FROGGY:
And you take one symphony listening to another symphony, why, like it might come on somewhere. But if your pad's not empty only because it's got things in it, then, brother, you're really hung up! Nobody's gonna dig no music with just the ears on the outside of his head!
AUNT CLEOBEL:
Because as more and more is offered without love, the area we can have real lives in grows smaller and smaller.
JOAN:
Until finally the only genuine feeling left to us is that we are not capable of feeling anything any more.
GERALD:
We can hire us up the boys with the cyclotron part in their hair to show us that the king hasn't got any clothes on—in compatible color on a screen so wide that every button looks like a blow-up of all the continents rolled into one big fiery mushroom; but nobody seems to care or to notice that somewhere along the line the king just kind of disappeared too. No clothes, no king, no nothin'.
OLD HORACE:
A fool went out to this garden and he met a couple fellahs leading a sort of a cow on a rope. The cow was not much bigger than a mosquito's handshake, but it had a horn in the middle of its forehead and the fool wondered how come they didn't stop it from eating everything in sight.
MRS. WORTHCROFT:
At first it was so small that it could eat the green without even disturbing the grass.

MR. WORTHCROFT:
  And its horn was so short that it took all three fellows looking all at once to even see it.
JOAN:
  But as the fool watched, the strange little animal began to get bigger and bigger...
GERALD:
  And before long it had devoured almost everything in the garden.
MRS. WORTHCROFT:
  So the fool said to them...
  (*There is another pause.* OLD HORACE *lowers his head; the music comes to a sudden stop; then, while the others stand frozen, he slowly raises his head—and the jazz comes on swinging... swinging hard.*)
  (*Fast beat*)
FROGGY:
  Like this turtle with the beat alto on top, he lombardos through the carrots and all that, you got yourself a spooky scene; but you're a couple real heat city busters if you let him split without a say-who to those cats out there blowing some great piano. Like nobody will make it.
GERALD:
  Warn them? How can we warn them? If the boss has something wrapped to sell as a dairy package, and in the stamping machine maybe some dragon feathers get added, you fire one guy that don't make it unstick; you've got to chop the whole department. And don't forget, there ain't nobody don't work here.
MR. WORTHCROFT:
  You ask us to tell the good people to keep their doors and windows locked; sure, but the only ones we'd really tip off are the boys who go around seeing to it that nobody's house is ever closed to the damn thing!
FROGGY:
  But where do you stand? Like the yak sounds so good, you

don't have to say anything. I hear you come on, but I don't ever hear where you been.

GERALD:
So? If maybe the boss merchandises a model where, say, one of the bugs in it, once it gets off the drawingboard, turns into sort of lamb that not only follows Mary to school but also sinks his choppers into all her little playmates, and then proceeds to chase teacher up a certain well-known creek—

FROGGY *(interrupting)*:
But where do you stand? Like nobody wants to cut this take. The tune's all shoes and no feet. Only thing anybody ever squared with a square was a big empty box with his own name plastered all over it.

MRS. WORTHCROFT:
Meanwhile, back at the mansion the butler was getting all set to bump off none other than the Author of our little story! Poor God, He never had a chance; much too set in His ways—why, I'll bet you a handful of solar systems that He couldn't even qualify to get into one of those Institutes for Advanced Studies!

AUNT CLEOBEL:
Ignorance is evil: but knowledge that is turned against itself, against men, and against God, is an abomination for which a new word must be made. And if ever that word does come to be spoken—in all its terrible horror—nothing that is alive now will be left to hear it.

(There is a pause; and the music lowers.)

OLD HORACE:
Sometimes a man looks up at the stars, he sort of wishes he had him something to clean his eyes with.

JOAN:
It fades. The dress of the bride is a shroud.

GERALD:
And the groom has bloody sweat in his hair. Ah, this is a nasty stretch of part to be going through on a night like this.

MR. WORTHCROFT:
And the driver mad as a man among men.

MRS. WORTHCROFT:
  Ah, men. Thought I'd bought a rooster, but it's not even a very good hen.
OLD HORACE *(beginning a slow shuffling dance)*:
  How do you want your cannonballs, boomy side up?
  (The music comes on driving once more.)
FROGGY *(beginning to snap his fingers)*:
  Like you ride their trolley, man, you don't have to get off at hell—you've been there all the time.
OLD HORACE:
  Tell me something. You see a man comin' round here lately has a sort of a dog on a stick?
FROGGY:
  How long ago, man?
OLD HORACE:
  Oh, 'bout like this. *(Indicating a height with his hand.)*
FROGGY *(doing a slow knee flex)*:
  Why, no, but I had an uncle he could surround 'surround' so you tried to get your arm through you had to take all the pegs out first.
OLD HORACE:
  You might not of noticed him. He was sort of a governor before somebody paved the street over him.
FROGGY:
  You mean this cat with the stick?
OLD HORACE:
  No, I mean this sort of hounddawg. You couldn't miss him, had his pants on over his clothes.
FROGGY:
  One time my uncle he hesitated so hard—you know, getting out of his bed—he was downtown two hours before it even occurred to him that he wasn't up yet.
  (The others are standing quietly; their heads turning mechanically from one speaker to the other.)
OLD HORACE:
  You don't happen to have a bottle on you, do you, boy?
FROGGY:
  I suppose you want some juice?

OLD HORACE:
Hell, no, what would I want a drink for? I just want to see if my neck leaks.
FROGGY:
Reminds me when I was a baby my mother got so she had to feed me nothing but garlic.
OLD HORACE:
What's the matter, did you have the worms, boy?
FROGGY:
No. The reason she did that, I kept getting lost in grandpa's beard all the time.
OLD HORACE:
My fourth wife had a mouth so big, why, she could sing quartets all by herself! Smart woman, too—had a fancy sign in the window that said: Haircuts while you wait.
FROGGY:
All the rest have thirty-one, except the Bobby Twins—they got so sweet, so cold, and so *bare*— why, man, they used to walk up in the elevator and ride down on the stair!
OLD HORACE:
You know, the soberer I stand here, the longer I feel.
FROGGY:
What's the juice for a quick gander, lays on the bug if you look at it awhile.
OLD HORACE:
Yep. Sometimes takes more'n two pints to make one cavort.
FROGGY:
Like I'd say to Mary Belle, there'd be more of us of use around here if you'd get your old man to go off into that other room-like.
OLD HORACE:
When I was courtin' my sixth wife, I'd sometimes have to borrow my third wife's car because my fifth wife was too stingy to lend me cabfare.
FROGGY:
You'd maybe think that chick could dig the scene—like she could tell you a bit of this and a bit of that. Like you're

walking into one of these grocery stores and there's a box of some new soap product or maybe a can of peaches, say, on the floor; you know, like you've got yourself a scene in some lousy furnished pad, with a hotplate smeared all over with burnt eggs and stuff, and you been around... Like some good Joe comes in and he's cryin' with real tears, like a small kid, and so when you tell him, Look, like we're all defeated—and he knows that you don't know him... like maybe nobody knows anybody, and it doesn't matter, because it's not because of any of that. I mean, if you can't kid yourself, you got to keep making the scene because you know the rain comes down-like, and maybe some little mutt's got a busted leg, and maybe you hear a dirty old bum-like telling the fuzzy that Jesus will look after them, and it's the old bum's got his shirt torn off and his beard like some shredded wheat dunked in red paint. Like all that doesn't matter; you hear the man talk, and it don't translate. But, anyway, Mary Belle would pick up on the store bit, like maybe you see some people buying stuff and they're going to cart it home and take it out of the bag and maybe say, "I think we got overcharged on these grapefruits." I mean, can you imagine being serious about a thing like that! "I think we got, we got overcharged on these grapefruits!"

OLD HORACE:
Not being a married man myself, I guess you might say that it wouldn't surprise me much to find a bit of sauerkraut stuck at the bottom of the milk pitcher.

FROGGY:
Took me a long time to realize that she actually believed if you had, say, enough sticks of bread you could maybe leave one place and go to another place. I mean, she *actually* believed it! Now, like nobody can swing would believe a thing like that!

OLD HORACE:
I remember in Philly we used to roll the people up at night so the sidewalks could have some fun.

FROGGY:
> What I think is, if somebody has to curl up on the belly of a lot of homogenized hakkity-yak before he can feel anything, then his scene's folded right there.

OLD HORACE:
> Now you take this friend of mine. One day he walks into the mayor's office and he says: "Boy, you're so dumb I brought you some smart pills." The Mayor is sort of surprised, see; so he puts a couple in his mouth. Then he starts to spit and holler; "Get this fellah outta here! Smart pills? Why, that's nothing but pieces of bird-dirt!" So as they're a-draggin' him out, this friend of mine says: "What did I tell you? They're startin' to work already."

FROGGY:
> It breaks down to: some can swing; and some got the lights turned out—like the only scene for them is when the devil comes to collect on the light bill, and they can't even see who it is!

OLD HORACE:
> But when you stop to think of it, if the good fellah's gonna stay in business at all, he can't be in business for just himself—because if his store ain't set up for the bad fellah, it don't make any sense for him to stand 'round tryin' to sell himself something he's already bought a closetful of.

FROGGY:
> But no matter what you got in there to show somebody, if the lights are all out, who's gonna see it? Like maybe you've booked like an angel even, and he blows so you could walk right on it up to the door where the man says all that yak and stuff has got some truth in it—and everybody in the world is sitting at the same table, like nobody gets put down for any of that jive-like... like up to now, that's all been a lousy lie!—and you're glad nobody can see him! You're glad the lights are out! Because if the good citizens are good at anything, they're sure good at putting the fold on a hard swinger!

AUNT CLEOBEL (*slowly as the music lowers*):
> Dark and light divide our lives on the level of our most

common existence. The day does follow the night—and we have only to believe this miracle. All the others follow it. And if men doubt what their experience knows, they are not onlyey are mad.

MRS. WORTHCROFT *(spelling it out)*:
M-a-d.

MR. WORTHCROFT:
D-a-m.

GERALD:
What is it goes 'round locking everybody up so they can be f-r-e-e?

(There is a long pause while they all stand very still. Then JOAN *leans over and whispers something to* GERALD, *who laughs and whispers something to* OLD HORACE, *who laughs and whispers something to* FROGGY, *who laughs and whispers something to* MRS. WORTHCROFT. *While this is going on the lights in the tablelamps overhead—unnoticed by anyone—go out; and the music comes up ... swinging for keeps now.* AUNT CLEOBEL *stands near the ceiling globe ... and its frosted glass etches the scene in a cold, hard light.)*

AUNT CLEOBEL:
Stop! It isn't too late! There is still time for us to love one another! There is still time ...!

(The cycle of whispering followed by laughter is repeated; this time beginning where it left off.)

It isn't too late! Don't you see that—*(She breaks off as the laughter gets louder.)*

OLD HORACE *(through the laughter)*:
Oh, there's a lot of it.

MR. WORTHCROFT:
A bit here, and a bit there.

GERALD:
All those kinds of this and that.

MRS. WORTHCROFT:
For every taste, you might say.

JOAN:
If you get born somebody you don't care for, that doesn't

matter; there are plenty of people around willing to live your life for you.

FROGGY:
Maybe they're a little mad-like, but you know how it goes.

GERALD:
That's how the sub versives itself when the captain leaves the hatch open-like.

MRS. WORTHCROFT:
My mother used to say, Well, here it is Tuesday; wouldn't surprise me if we'd be stuck with Wednesday again tomorrow.

MR. WORTHCROFT:
We had a neighbor one time, a Mrs. Johnson, the kind of woman you'd probably find she had a bald head if you shaved off enough of her hair; a little skinny, shy person— you know, she'd actually put a dress and shoes on before she'd even go into the street!

JOAN:
Then there are all those heroes with names like the chapters of books; and you never somehow expect them to care much about reading the type of story they're in.

OLD HORACE:
In the long run, the train that stands still will get where it is first.

GERALD:
We can save a lot of wear and tear in the pro and con department if we reach our decision and then find out what we're supposed to be deciding.

FROGGY:
Like maybe one guy don't even know the name of your street, and some other guy's even got the house number; but that other guy's so square, like he'd never dig the fact that he's lookin' for you in the wrong country!

AUNT CLEOBEL:
It isn't too late! The day *does* follow the night! We need not become what we are afraid of!

GERALD:
Ah, so beautiful! so true! the monkey said hee-haw!—and the lark said moo!

MR. WORTHCROFT:
  I wish I was a bull with wings, I wouldn't care whose damn blackboard I built my nest on.
JOAN:
  You've gone to a lot of trouble to show me your sleight of hand, but all I see is your thick head.
OLD HORACE:
  They ever find who she was? You know, that gal Sylvia?
MRS. WORTHCROFT:
  She's running a laundry in Scranton, or some such place farrago from here.
FROGGY:
  Don't you give up on me Virginia! Don't know I'll make it, but I'm comin' on, baby! You hear me, baby? Yeah, Virginia, all those big crocodile fir trees up there, with the sunset splashin' the snow with blood. Yeah, baby, I really do hate to see that sun go down. I really hate to see that sun go down.
GERALD:
  Take an awful lot of blackbirds to say the kind of goodbyes should get said around here now.
AUNT CLEOBEL:
  It's not too late! Oh, it's not too late! The heart of man is not dead! We only imagine this doorless cell, this tomb filling with darkness! Oh please stop! Stop!
MR. WORTHCROFT:
  It's all so touching, so very fey! The stars went plipptyplop, and Georgie Porgy just rotted away.
JOAN:
  Nightshade and wolfblade; silhouette and fife; if you can't even give me a lousy time, how come you give me a life?
AUNT CLEOBEL:
  Stop! Stop! The light will come! You must have faith!
GERALD:
  And why not pray tell? For faith, hope, and charity have gone out to sea in an atom-powered supercarrier; and if Little Red Riding Hood's grandmother is still listening, tell her the less we see of her the merrier.
MRS. WORTHCROFT:
  The boat stood on the burning deck; its fleece was wan as

Little Willie's sister—and if she hadn't jumped we wouldn't have missed her.

OLD HORACE:
There was once a fellah chased himself 'round and 'round a big field. And so a mouse clumb up on his front fender and ask him for a chaw of tebaccer. But his mother was somebody high up in the navy and he thought it must be a telegram saying she'd fallen off again; so he gives the horse a pat on the shoulder—you see, there were two horses, and it was only this *other one* was a mouse—and they all five had different last names. *(He pauses.)* How tall were they?

GERALD:
Oh, that's easy. The middle one was three inches shorter than the second tallest—give or take a couple hundred feet, depending on the distance from sea level.

AUNT CLEOBEL:
Oh, please! All of you! Won't you please stop! Please!

JOAN:
Oh, the owl knelt down on his selfish little knees; but the morning glory she didn't even bother to say she was sorry.

MR. WORTHCROFT:
Doorknobs, moonstones, and peppermint-flavored minks; it don't matter what you do to us, long's you don't clog up our sinks.

OLD HORACE:
I wonder, does that kind of stuff still go do do you suppose? You know, the birch and the white pine tree?

MRS. WORTHCROFT:
And the magnolia?

FROGGY:
And all that crazy moss-like in the big marble pots in front of those swank joints uptown?

GERALD:
And people going into shops in the evening and coming out with a lion's head of chrysanthemums in their purple arms?

JOAN:
And are there girls still with names like Candy Jean and Susan, Jill, Grace, Hazel, Angela, and Cora Ann?

FROGGY:
And do people actually still live in places like North Adams, Mass., and Detroit, White Plains, Buffalo, Erie, P.A., Abilene, Phoenix, El Paso, Galveston, Cedar Rapids, Chicago, Jacksonville? I mean do you think that's possible?
MR. WORTHCROFT:
Not to mention Hong Kong and London, Berlin, Amsterdam, Athens, Rome, Paris France, Moscow, Mexico City, Helsinki, and the lot.
MRS. WORTHCROFT:
And kitchen mops.
GERALD:
And sparkling waterfalls.
JOAN:
Daybeds and tiled bathrooms.
OLD HORACE:
Bones for the dog.
FROGGY:
Cats for Newcastle.
GERALD:
What the bricklayer said to the pastry cook.
JOAN:
What Mrs. Green said to her son Tom.
MRS. WORTHCROFT:
What Mrs. Withers did with the message from Garcia.
MR. WORTHCROFT:
Come, come, my pretty little quince pie.
OLD HORACE:
How big is 'high'?
GERALD:
Ha! and I know even less of other matters; that's why they elected me.
JOAN:
What a fool, that Manet—painting his "Lunch on the Grass."
OLD HORACE:
It takes jack to even get up a steeple.

MR. WORTHCROFT:
  Bring me some more of that gorgeous soup! Go on! go on! give me a real good splashing this time!
OLD HORACE:
  A Henny-Penny for your thoughts.
MR. WORTHCROFT:
  Oh, when flowerhood was in night, and the deep ran away with the soon.
    (AUNT CLEOBEL *is standing with bowed head near the globe—a few feet behind them.*)
OLD HORACE:
  A is for the alephant; B is for the honey.
JOAN:
  C is for what. And all the rest of the pretty talk.
GERALD:
  Mock. Meadow. Mask.
MRS. WORTHCROFT:
  Sack. Sparrow. Seed.
MR. WORTHCROFT:
  Bleed. Bower. Break.
GERALD:
  Fake. Fall. Famine.
FROGGY (*calling to* AUNT CLEOBEL):
  Lady!
MR. WORTHCROFT:
  One, four; shut the door.
FROGGY (*calling again*):
  Lady!
    (*The others remain motionless in their positions as* FROGGY *steps back to stand beside* AUNT CLEOBEL; *he can be seen—but not heard—talking to her.*)
GERALD (*slowly, speaking as one asleep*):
  The time is dying. Now there are only moments left.
    (*The light in the globe flickers off and on several times, then burns steadily again.* FROGGY *gently leads* AUNT CLEOBEL *forward into the group; the others turn like sleep-walkers as they approach.*)

FROGGY (*wonderingly, his eyes moving from face to face*):
 You know, back there, just now, I knew she couldn't hear me—and ... and for the first time in my life, I felt like ... you know, sometimes I sort-of-well, felt like I could tell someone. Really tell someone. Like I could say ... you know, like ... like it blows ... like it like it all blows ... only you don't mean that ... because if you only mean that, you ... you don't don't do your share ... you figure to let ... to let the cat upstairs do all your swinging for you ... and man ... man, we all got to make the scene together, or ... or before long there just won't be any scene left for anybody to make.
 (*There is a pause.*
 Then the music comes on like a storm—as they stand motionless, very close to one another—and after a long moment, the music abruptly stops.
 There is another pause.)
JOAN (*speaking without emotion, to* AUNT CLEOBEL):
 Why are you crying?
 (*Another pause.*)
MRS. WORTHCROFT (*in the same emotionless way*):
 What are we doing here?
MR. WORTHCROFT (*in the same emotionless way*):
 Yes, what are we doing here?
 (*Another pause. The light flickers again; but does not go out.*)
GERALD (*slowly*):
 One, two, three ...
OLD HORACE (*in the same emotionless way*):
 Why are you doing that? What are you counting for?
GERALD:
 Six, seven ... If anyone has anything to say, they better say it now. Nine ... Speak! Speak! It's the last chance!
 (*They all turn slowly, unbelievingly, to face the front.*)
 (*Then—after a moment, they are all speaking at once ... imploringly ... to the invisible wall before them. But nothing they say is heard. The silence grows in intensity for a moment. The light goes out. And after another long moment, the curtain comes down on the darkness.*)

Photo: Harry Redl

Photo: *William Wareing*

Photo: Harry Redl

THE CITY
WEARS A SLOUCH HAT

THE VOICE *(Sound of taxies, muffled clang of streetcars, etc.)*:
   Mm, it's beginning to rain a little. We'll just move back here into this doorway. There ... that's better.
MAN *(passing)*:
   Honest, kid, I didn't mean to say it.
WOMAN:
   You and your apologies! Phooey! How come every time we get to mother's you have to start in ...? *(Trails off)*
THE VOICE:
   Yeah ... that's the way it is.
      (Somebody whistling: "My Bonnie Lies Over the Ocean")
THE VOICE:
   Da da da da da da da di di ...
MAN:
   Say, buddie, yuh got something t' spare a fellah ... I ain't eaten since yesterday.
VOICE:
   Sure. Here.
MAN:
   Thanks. Hate t' bother but I ... *(Moves off)*
VOICE *(as siren screams out on street)*:
   Say ... let's have a look. *(Sound of trucks, sirens, etc.)*

VOICE:
'Ah, it's just an old pile of rags in the alley!' 'Can't be too careful around these old buildings.' *(Trails off)*
VOICE:
Yuh... Say, that rain's really beginning to come down. I'm going to duck back under this awning.
WOMAN:
And a dozen oranges.
MAN:
These?—or the navels?
WOMAN:
I want them for juice.
MAN:
Oh. A dozen, you say?
WOMAN:
Yes... and I want a bunch of celery, three pounds of your best tomatoes...
THE VOICE *(moving away)*:
We'd better find another spot. Ah... this looks well out of the weather.
MAN:
Stick 'em up, Jack.
VOICE:
They're up.
MAN:
Fork over.
VOICE:
Here we are... my wallet, my wrist watch...
MAN:
Now don't try anything fancy. I'd as soon plug you as breathe.
VOICE:
I bet you would. Here, I think that's all.
MAN:
You're a smart fellah. Well, be seein' yuh.
VOICE:
Just a minute. You won't have any use for the cards and the photograph in my wallet... return them to me, please.

MAN:
> Ah ... O.K. I ain't got no use for 'em. Here yuh are.

VOICE:
> Thank you very much. Goodnight.

MAN:
> So long. *(Pause. Calling back)* Hey! Whose pic've you got there? Yer wife? Maybe yer mother?

VOICE:
> No.

MAN:
> O.K. bud. Keep yer little secret.

VOICE:
> It's no secret. It's your picture.

MAN *(coming up)*:
> What! Say, what yuh handin' me?

VOICE:
> Here, look for yourself.

MAN *(after pause)*:
> Jeese ... *(frightened)* Look, guy, here, take your money. I don't wanta get mixed up in nothin' like that.

VOICE:
> Like what? Don't be a fool. I can't stand all night here in the rain talking to you. Goodnight.

MAN:
> But I don't want ...

THE VOICE:
> I can't help what you want. *(Pause—walking)* Brr ... That wind's beginning to go right through me. What I need's a little good cheer.

MAN:
> Yes sir.

VOICE:
> Nice crowd tonight.

MAN:
> Pretty good.

WOMAN:
> Good evening, sir.

VOICE:
> Good evening. Wait, I'll take my cigarettes out of the coat first.

WOMAN:
> Here's your check, sir.

VOICE:
> Thank you.

MAN:
> Good evening. Table?

VOICE *(through a boogie woogie piano)*:
> No, I'll just stand here.

MAN:
> What'll you have?

VOICE:
> Oh... let's see... Give me a bit of that.

MAN *(clinking bottle)*:
> This, sir?

VOICE:
> That's right... go easy on the lemon.

MAN *(passing)*:
> Listen, Al, that nannie goat couldn't win a race if they put snowshoes on the other gees.

AL:
> Have it your way. *(Hubbub of talk dies away as boogie woogie ends)*

M.C.:
> And now, ladies and gentlemen, I'd like to introduce you to a little lady...

THE VOICE *(street noises)*:
> I don't care much for her voice.

BOY:
> Paper! Paper! Paper, mister?

VOICE:
> No, I don't want a paper.

MAN:
> Here, give me one. Here you are. *(Moving off)* Now, Ed, you know as well as I do that a thing like that can cause a lot of trouble.

ED:
But I still think you could make something out of it. Why, there were ... *(Trails off)*
VOICE:
That sounds like it might be interesting. We'll see.
MAN:
A dog maybe, but not a horse.
ED:
What's the matter with a horse?
MAN:
There ain't nothing the matter with a horse, but if it was a dog I'd feel a lot better.
ED:
O.K., you'd feel better, but that horse ain't a dog. *(Pause—snap of a match)* Go ahead, light yer own first. *(Pause)* What's Ida think?
MAN:
What's Ida think? What d'you think she thinks. There we are ... in the kitchen ... playin' cards with the neighbors in the front room ... it don't make no difference to him ... he'll just mosey in and start talkin'.
ED:
What's he say?
MAN:
What's he say? What don't he say? That horse just pops out with the first thing comes in his head.
ED:
I still think you could make something out of him. Why, I'll bet a lot of people ...
THE VOICE:
Ah, well ... They walk too fast. *(Pause)* It might be nice to stroll along the river for a bit. *(Sound of fog horns)* I can't get much wetter.
MAN:
Huh?
THE VOICE:
I just said I couldn't get much wetter.

MAN:
Oh, that's all right.
VOICE:
Good of you to say so. What are you doing sitting down here in the rain?
MAN:
Oh, just listening to the boats.
VOICE:
It's nice all right.
MAN:
You ever been up in an airplane?
VOICE:
Yes, several times. Why?
MAN:
I always wanted to see what things look like from up there. Pretty good, eh?
VOICE:
Pretty good.
MAN:
You ever been in Mellyberg?
VOICE:
Where's Mellyberg?
MAN:
I'm not sure ... think it's somewhere along the Dan.
VOICE:
The Dan ... What's the Dan?
MAN:
It's a lake near Blodget City ... up near the border.
VOICE:
Well, I hope you get your wish.
MAN:
What wish?
VOICE:
To go up in a plane.
MAN:
Yeah, I do too. *(Pause)* You ever been in any them creameries near Mellyberg?

VOICE:
Yes, I went all through one about a week ago.
MAN:
The Johnson boy still work there?
VOICE:
Which one? Tom?
MAN:
No, Freddie.
VOICE:
Freddie quit the day before I went there.
MAN:
Was that a Wednesday?
VOICE:
Friday.
MAN:
Mm... *(Pause)* You ever plant any rice?
VOICE:
No, I never did. Do you see the light in that big apartment house over there?—Up about six floors.
MAN:
Sure, I see it.
VOICE:
I think I'll go up and answer the phone. *(Pause) (Phone ringing)* Hello. No, they went out to Bill's sister's... Couldn't say exactly, but I don't think you should wait for them to come in. *(Pause)* Yuh, that's right... you'd have a rather long wait... you see, the pavement's pretty wet tonight, and their car is going to skid off into a tree... all of them, even the baby... the car'll catch fire... Yes, just ten minutes from now. *(Pause)* It doesn't matter how I know... I'm sorry. Goodnight. *(Pause) (Taxi horn)* Feels good to get some fresh air again.
MAN:
Look, buddie... you know them three guys back there?
VOICE:
Which?

MAN:
Them back near the candy store. They been followin' yuh ever since yuh left your house.
VOICE:
They have...? How do you know?
MAN:
How do you suppose?
VOICE:
And why were you following me?
MAN:
I didn't have nothin else to do.
VOICE:
Maybe they feel the same way.
MAN:
But I ain't packin' no gun like they are.
VOICE:
O.K. Thanks. I'll wait until they come up. *(Pause)* Hello, boys, anything I can do for you?
FIRST:
Not a thing.
SECOND:
What'd he tell you?
VOICE:
Who? What'd who tell me?
FIRST:
The guy you were just talkin' to.
VOICE:
Oh... why, he said you three were following me.
SECOND *(laughing)*:
He told you that, eh?
THIRD *(deep voice)*:
Come on, Spool, first thing you know he'll give us the slip.
SECOND:
Right. The dirty rat!
VOICE:
What's he done to you?
THIRD:
If we wanted you to know, dickie-bird, we'd tell you.

SECOND *(sound of a blow being struck, scuffle)*:
Cripes! Out like a light.
FIRST:
What the hell! Why'd yuh hit him?
VOICE:
I don't like to be called dickie-bird. Pick up your friend, and get on your way.
SECOND:
Why, you ... we oughta plug yuh ...
VOICE:
You can't very well do that with empty revolvers.
SECOND:
Empty? *(Click, click, as cylinder is rolled)* Now how the ...
THIRD:
Come on, let's get outta here.
VOICE:
So long, Tinkins, Sloane and O'Malley.
FIRST:
Wait a minute. How'd you know our names?
VOICE:
Are they?
THIRD:
Jeese ... say, them ain't our names.
   (Rumble of thunder, roll continues)
VOICE:
That reminds me. Let's walk up and look around in the sky a bit. *(Sound for two or three minutes)* I wonder what that strange-looking creature is over there on that big cloud. *(Strange sound)* Mm ... seems to be trying to say something to me. *(Loud crash of thunder)* We'd better get back down, I guess.
WOMAN:
Hello.
VOICE:
Hello.
WOMAN:
Do you mind if I talk to you?

VOICE:
>Not at all. But perhaps we should get in somewhere out of the rain . . . there's a lunch room just across the street.

WOMAN:
>No, I like it here. I don't want to go anywhere where there's light . . . where people can see me . . .

VOICE:
>But why?

WOMAN *(near hysteria)*:
>I'm ugly! It's not fair! Not fair I tell you! I . . . I . . . *(Begins to sob)*

VOICE:
>Come now, that won't help. Nothing is ever as terrible as we think it is. Your face is scarred?

WOMAN *(through sobs)*:
>Yes . . . I can't go on this way. I have nothing to live for now. *(Sobs weakly)* Everything . . . all of it . . . our plans . . . the life we could have had together . . .

VOICE:
>Does he know where you are?

WOMAN *(shortly)*:
>No.

VOICE:
>Don't you think . . .

WOMAN:
>No, No . . . he must never know . . . it would kill him if he knew.

VOICE:
>But if he loves you . . .

WOMAN *(bitterly)*:
>Love! How long do you think his love would last when he saw . . . when he . . . *(Sobs)*

VOICE:
>When did this happen?

WOMAN:
>Four months ago. I was moving a plate-glass mirror in my apartment . . . I . . . I fell, and it . . . the . . .

The City Wears a Slouch Hat

VOICE:
  Can't the doctors help you? There have been some wonderful developments in surgery during the past few years.
WOMAN:
  No. Nothing can be done. Please ... please ... don't light your cigarette ...
VOICE *(striking match)*:
  I see.
WOMAN:
  Now are you satisfied?
VOICE:
  But why ... ?
WOMAN:
  Do you begin to understand now why I can't go back to him? Why I can't ...
VOICE:
  Why did you lie to me? Why did you tell me your face was scarred, disfigured?
WOMAN:
  I knew it was useless to talk to you. No one can understand—Blind! You blind fools! Fools! Fools! *(Fades, sobbing)* *(Sound of brakes as car comes to curb)*
MAN:
  That's him.
ANOTHER *(scuffle)*:
  I got him. Give us a hand, Sam.
VOICE *(muffled, as through gag)*:
  Who are you? What do you want? *(Click of car door, motor up as car begins to move)*
MAN *(singing throatily)*:
  My bonnie lies over de ocean, etc.
ANOTHER:
  Pipe down, Sam, you'll wake the baby. *(Baby cries fretfully)* What'd I tell yuh?
MAN:
  Ah right, so let it squawk. *(Baby cries louder as car noise reaches peak—Sam sings through—after a moment, brakes are suddenly applied)*

ANOTHER:
O.K. bub, here we are. Get out. *(Car immediately starts, fade of motor)*
VOICE:
Mm . . . here we are back where we started from. *(Strange sound begins, softly at first, then louder)* I wonder what they're doing over there!
MAN:
Keep off. Stand back. Wanta get hurt?
VOICE:
But what's that for? That machine with all the big gold pipes?
MAN:
It's a mirthogram. Watch. Look what we can make it do . . . *(Noise up)* Now listen . . . *(Presently a little chuckle like a cackle)* There! Didn't I tell you!
VOICE:
But what use is it?
MAN:
What use is it? Did you ever hear a machine laugh before?
VOICE:
No, I suppose not. *(Pause)* It's funny what people will do. The great things and the dirty little things . . . *(Street sounds through following—silt of rain):*

> Come live with me and be my love,
> And we will all the pleasures prove
> That hills and valleys, dales and fields
> Or woods or steepy mountain yields.
>
> And we will sit upon the rocks,
> And see the shepherds feed their flocks
> By shallow rivers, to whose falls
> Melodious birds sing madrigals.
>
> And I will make thee beds of roses
> And a thousand fragrant posies;
> A cap of flowers, and a kirtle
> Embroider'd all with leaves of myrtle.

A gown made of the finest wool
Which from our pretty lambs we pull;
Fair-lined slippers for the cold,
With buckles of the purest gold.

(A police whistle—voices: Come on, move along, there, etc.)

A belt of straw and ivy-buds
With coral clasps and amber studs:
And if these pleasures may thee move,
Come live with me and be my love.

The shepherd swains shall dance and sing
For thy delight each May morning:
If these delights thy mind may move,
Then live with me and be my love.

(Scattered voices: "Say another one! I used to know that in school! Don't block the sidewalk; *etc.*—*Through reading of next poem instruments begin a rhythmic beat—sound of taxis, occasional voices, etc., continue.)*

Death, be not proud though some have called thee
Mighty and dreadful, for thou art not so:
For those whom thou think'st thou dost overthrow
Die not, poor Death; nor yet canst thou kill me.
From rest and sleep, which but thy picture be,
Much pleasure, then from thee much more must flow;
And soonest our best men with thee do go—
Rest of their bones and soul's delivery!
Thou'rt slave to fate, chance, kings, and desperate
  men,
And dost with poison, war, and sickness dwell;
And poppy or charms can make no sleep as well
And better than thy stroke. Why swell'st thou then?
One short sleep past, we wake eternally,
And death shall be no more: Death, thou shalt die!

(A silence)

THE VOICE* *(continuing)*:
   I think I'll go into this movie house here. Just one, please.
   (Sounds coming up on screen)
A MAN:
   You do love me ...
USHER:
   How far down, sir?
VOICE:
   This is all right.
A WOMAN:
   Of course I love you, Jason.
ANOTHER MAN:
   Do I interrupt anything?
MAN:
   No, D.J., your wife and I were just talking about the opera.
SECOND MAN:
   Oh.
WOMAN:
   Yes, Darius, Jason and I were arguing about Giglio Usipi.
MAN:
   Geraldine thinks he's greater than Felfior.
SECOND:
   And don't you?
MAN:
   It depends on the way you analyze their work.
WOMAN:
   But that's unimportant now. Will you have some tea, Darius.
SECOND:
   No, thanks, I just dropped in for a minute.
MAN:
   You're not going back to Dayton so soon, are you, D.J.?

---

*In the performance script, all lines from here to THE VOICE: " ... I'm sorry. I'm terribly sorry." are crossed out, most likely for reasons of time.

SECOND:
   Afraid I'll have to, old man. Got some things to look into at the Amalgamated. Good seeing both of you again.
MAN:
   Not at all.
WOMAN:
   You'll ring me up darling, when you're settled?
SECOND:
   I certainly shall.
   (Sound of door opening and clicking to)
MAN:
   I'm mad about you . . .
WOMAN:
   Stop, Jason, you're ruining my finger wave.
MAN *(suddenly, frightened)*:
   What was that?
WOMAN:
   Nothing, dear, probably the janitor collecting the garbage.
MAN:
   It sounded like somebody opening the window in the pantry. Sh . . .
   (Silence)
SECOND:
   Hope I didn't disturb you. I forgot my toothbrush.
WOMAN:
   It's on the stand near the door in your room.
SECOND *(leaving)*:
   Pip, pip.
MAN:
   Pip.
WOMAN:
   Do you think he suspects anything, Jason?
MAN:
   Who? D.J.? Why he wouldn't stoop to a thing like that.
WOMAN:
   Jason, honey . . .

MAN:
  Uh huh.
WOMAN:
  Do you remember that little diamond clip you gave me?
MAN:
  Last summer?
WOMAN:
  No, the time Darius went to Montreal.
MAN:
  Oh, that ... sure, Why?
WOMAN:
  It goes very nicely with my green outfit.
MAN:
  Well I'm glad.
WOMAN:
  And Jason ...
MAN:
  Yes.
WOMAN:
  I want to thank you for phoning Mrs. Semple for me.
MAN:
  Say no more about it.
WOMAN:
  Was she cross?
MAN:
  Not especially. She asked about Philip.
WOMAN:
  Poor Philip.
MAN:
  Is he going back to selling bonds?
WOMAN:
  No, Phil's coaching football at Plinith Hills.
MAN:
  You know I'm mad about you.
WOMAN:
  Did Mrs. Semple say who'd been at her party?

MAN:
  Oh, the usual bunch...
WOMAN:
  Jane Pellenger?
MAN:
  Let me think now... No, she didn't mention... Oh, yes she did... Jane came with Norbert Fisk.
WOMAN:
  No! Not Norbert Fisk.
MAN:
  That's what she said. Geraldine, we can't go on this way...
WOMAN:
  Why not?
MAN:
  But don't you see, sooner or later people will begin to talk and...
WOMAN:
  I should hope they're talking already.
MAN:
  But your children...
WOMAN:
  Oh, that... Randall never hears about anything at Yale, and Prissie is too self-centered to care much if her mother is made to suffer from the narrow-mindedness of people in our circle.
  (Loud snore)
MAN IN NEXT SEAT:
  I beg your pardon, but...
THE VOICE:
  ... I'm sorry. I'm terribly sorry.
  (Pause—street noises again)
  I'd like to be off somewhere listening to the ocean right now.
  (Thunder of waves breaking on shore) I'm going to swim out to that rock there. *(Sound of breathing through pounding of sea)* Ah... *(Exertion of pulling himself on rock)* I'll enjoy being alone... sort of tasting the juices of the night.

MAN:
It's nice out here, eh?
VOICE:
Huh! Oh ... What are you doing out on this rock in the ocean.
VOICE:
I live here.
VOICE:
You live here!?
MAN:
Yeah, for a long time now. I got sorta tired of things on the shore ... always the same ... men and women doing the same stupid things over and over ... and the noise of the city ... nah, it's good out here. Listen to her beatin' in. Just feel that good clean power surgin' in from the dark ... cruel, ruthless, old as time ... but listen to 'er ... she's drivin' in ... she knows what she wants ... There's no hero or devil on earth can talk back to her ... your little cardboard Napoleans, bah! Come on in, girl—roll 'em under ... Listen to her ... knock 'em down ... she'll be moving in here like a beautiful queen when all the little pains and deaths and conquests we know about are forgotten.
VOICE:
I know exactly what you mean. *(Begins to howl above the sound of the sea:* MAN *joins in)*
(A silence—suddenly)
I think we need more love in the world ... more understanding ... I want to know you ... what you believe ... what you feel ... what things among all the things you've heard about and known mean something to you ... we were not meant to be strangers to each other ... we have the same fears, the same hopes, joys and sorrows ... We must not be suspicious ... we must learn to love each other ... If

one man fails to believe, then there can be no faith in the world—for all men are finally one man, you, me—we cannot stand apart from each other. I am coming into your house with my hand outstretched. I am your friend. Do not be afraid of me.

*Designed by Marcia Burtt for
Capra Press in Santa Barbara,
October 1977. Typeset by
Charlene McAdams, printed by
Haagen Printing and bound by
Aaron Young. One hundred copies, numbered
and signed by the editor, were
handbound by Emily Paine.*